The Data Mirage

The Data Mirage

Why Companies Fail to Actually Use Their Data

Ruben Ugarte

BUSINESS EXPERT PRESS

Leader in applied, concise business books

The Data Mirage: Why Companies Fail to Actually Use Their Data

Cover design by Alison Davis

Interior design by Exeter Premedia Services Private Ltd., Chennai, India

First published in 2021 by
Business Expert Press, LLC
222 East 46th Street, New York, NY 10017
www.businessexpertpress.com

ISBN-13: 978-1-95334-952-1 (paperback)
ISBN-13: 978-1-95334-953-8 (e-book)

Business Expert Press Big Data, Business Analytics, and
Smart Technology Collection

Collection ISSN: 2333-6749 (print)
Collection ISSN: 2333-6757 (electronic)

First edition: 2021

10 9 8 7 6 5 4 3 2 1

To my parents, who have supported most of my crazy ideas including running my own business and being an entrepreneur. Thank you and I love you.

Description

The Data Mirage: Why Companies Fail to Actually Use Their Data is a business book for executives and leaders who want to unlock more insights from their data and make better decisions.

The importance of data doesn't need an introduction or a fancy pitch deck. Data plays a critical role in helping companies to better understand their users, beat out their competitors, and breakthrough their growth targets.

However, despite significant investments in their data, most organizations struggle to get much value from it. According to Forrester, only 38% of senior executives and decision-makers "have a high level of confidence in their customer insights and only 33% trust the analytics they generate from their business operations."

This reflects the real world that I have experienced. In this book, I will help readers formulate an analytics strategy that works in the real world, show them how to think about KPIs and help them tackle the problems they are bound to come across as they try to use data to make better decisions.

Keywords

analytics; marketing strategy; growth hacking; data; KPI; dashboards; data science; SaaS; e-commerce; mobile games; marketing attribution

Contents

Acknowledgements

Writing this book has been an exciting journey that couldn't have happened without many people's support. I want to thank my parents and sister for their continued encouragement to be a better person.

I also want to thank Alan Weiss and Noah Fleming, who helped shaped many of the ideas that made it into this book. I also want to thank the clients, colleagues, and partners who have been part of my practice over the last 5 years.

I also want to thank Scott, Charlene, and the rest of the BEP team for making the production of this book extremely easy. A special thanks to Exeter team for working with me through multiple iterations and fixes.

Finally, I want to thank Brian Yan Muk, Troy Liew, Tim Parkin, John Chan, and many other friends who provided feedback on the book cover, ideas, and overall structure. Apologies if I missed anyone and thank you for your support!

Introduction

The idea to write this book was in the back of my mind for four years. I kept seeing companies face the same challenges over and over again. These companies weren't able to find much information online or in books. Most of the content was focused on technical topics like choosing tools or how to design visually appealing reports.

The human element of data was surprisingly missing. After all, all this data that companies are drowning in is to be used by people. So why wasn't there more on how people use data or the challenges they face? My goal in this book is to help answer these questions.

You might assume that as a Data Strategist, I think data is the answer to every question. It might surprise you to know that I think companies are relying too much on data. I understand the power of it but I also respect its limitations. My work with clients has to be rooted in reality and not in a hypothetical world.

One of the first questions that I share with clients is what game are they playing? I want them to understand that there are different ways of approaching data and no single approach is the "best." Every company has a unique makeup of skills and preferences (what we might call culture) and data needs to be fit into this mold.

The most well-known data game is played by companies like Facebook and Google. They collect vast amounts of data which they then use to build better products. Better in this case means higher engagement from their users (you and me). Their approach to data is sophisticated, complex, and effective.

This is one game you could play. For these companies, data is their product and they monetize it through advertising. Everything else they do is meant to support this. Facebook has a social networking tool, Whatsapp, Instagram, and Messenger, which could be seen as "products" but they are all just ways in which Facebook collects data.

Google is the same. They offer free products like Gmail, Google Maps, Android, and Google Home. However, these products are just a way for them to collect data. If you don't believe me, let's look at recent quarterly results for these companies. Advertising was 98 percent[1] of Facebook's revenue and 83 percent[2] of Google's revenue in 2019.

Unless you're building a similar business to Google and Facebook, this game might not be a good fit. This means that you don't need to make data the most important thing in your company. You don't need to be "data-driven" and have data guide your every decision. Instead, you could explore other games.

I believe most companies will benefit from a "data-supported culture." This means that data plays an important role in helping you make better decisions but there's also room for opinions and gut feelings. If you don't have the data on a certain question, you can still make a decision. You aren't paralyzed by the lack of evidence.

This last point is important because I have seen companies delay decisions until "all the data is in." I understand prudence but there are also limitations to this approach. Instead, companies should focus on building a data strategy that helps them achieve their goals while balancing the reality of internal capabilities.

In this book, I will take you through the entire lifecycle of a data strategy. We'll define the ideal future, get people onboard, choose the right technology, implement it, provide training, and mine the data for insights. I'll show you best practices along the way that I have learned from working with over 75+ companies across multiple industries and 5 continents. The principles are quite similar regardless of what your company offers.

Finally, I will help you increase the confidence in your data and the decisions that you're making. At the end of the day, I'm here (and clients hire me) to help them grow their businesses.

Let's start our journey.
Ruben Ugarte,
Vancouver, Canada
June 2020

---

[1] https://investor.fb.com/investor-news/press-release-details/2020/Facebook-Reports-First-Quarter-2020-Results/default.aspx
[2] https://forbes.com/sites/greatspeculations/2020/05/18/10-billion-googles-lost-advertising-revenues-due-to-the-covid-19-outbreak/#54bf0fba6f46

CHAPTER 1

The Reality of Being Data Driven and Why Your Company Isn't

The only way to make sense out of change is to plunge into it, move with it, and join the dance.

—Alan Wilson Watts

There were dashboards everywhere,[1] monitoring activity across the network and showing the latest news from CNN, MSNBC, and Fox News. If anything unusual happened, you would instantly see it on one of the monitors. The company could then respond right away and prevent any serious consequences.

This was the "War Room" that Facebook had set up to monitor the U.S. midterm elections in 2018. The company has built special dashboards to monitor fake news, bots trying to spread misinformation, and nefarious actors.

This might seem over the top for Facebook but the company has been under ever-increasing pressure for its role in the 2016 U.S. presidential election. It had become public that foreign organizations were able to use Facebook to influence the outcome of that election. The "War Room" was a response to all of this but it is unclear if it will be enough.

Facebook is an extreme example of a company that uses data to make decisions. The company uses this data to show you exactly what you care about when you browse your newsfeed and hopes that you stick around for longer than necessary. Their data-driven decisions work. In 2019,

---

[1] "Inside Facebook's Election 'War Room'." *Technology News, The New York Times,* https://nytimes.com/2018/09/19/technology/facebook-election-war-room.html (accessed September 19, 2018).

1.62 billion people used one of its products on a daily basis[2] including Whatsapp, Instagram, or Messenger.

While most companies will never reach the level Facebook has, it does show the potential impact that data can have on any organization. This book is your guide to getting more value out of your data.

You don't need to go to the same level Facebook has. For them, data is their business. Everything else is mostly there to support the collection of data. For other businesses, data is meant to support your core value which could be products or services.

In this book, we'll look at everything you need to do to get data right. Let's start our journey at the beginning, by providing context.

Let's Start at the Beginning

Every great story has a beginning and, for companies that are striving to be data driven, the beginning can feel like a failure. Every single one of my clients tells me that that they would like to go from nothing to advanced as quickly as possible. They want to skip the beginning and jump to the end of the story.

They assume (rightly so) that they aren't limited by technology. We have advanced computers that fit into our pants and self-driving cars. I'm sure we can figure out how our customers engage with our products. The latter seems simplistic in comparison to other technologies.

The mistake is to assume that we are talking about technical problems. In this book, we'll talk about tools, machine learning models, and other technical ideas but I don't think they are the main issues that companies need to solve.

Instead, my experience over the past five years tells me that the biggest challenges are related to people and psychology. These issues manifest when your team tells you that they don't trust the data or when they outright reject a number because "it can't be right."

---

[2] "We Just Shared our Community Update." *Facebook Post*, Facebook, https://facebook.com/zuck/posts/10107243286682221 (accessed on April 24, 2019).

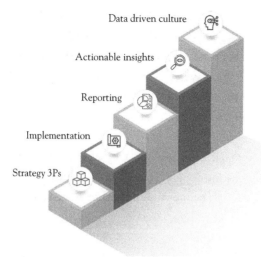

Figure 1.1 Data Adoption Lifecycle (DAL)

A mentor once told me that we should always look for "cause, not blame."[3] Blaming people isn't the solution. Instead, we need to diagnose why this lack of trust exists or why it seems that some teams are unable to actually use the data they have.

This is the journey that we will take in this book. I'll give you the best tools for your product or industry, show how advanced techniques like machine learning can help your business, and demystify data science into practical applications. This is what companies want when they reach out to me but it isn't always what they need.

Diagnosing this gap between want and need is sometimes tricky. To help prospects understand it, I use a simple model that I call the "Data Adoption Lifecycle (DAL)" (Figure 1.1).

Everything starts with the strategy which we will cover in Chapter 2. Once we have a plan that makes sense, we can move on to the implementation which we will cover in Chapters 3 and 4. After collecting data, we can go through a reporting phase which we will cover in Chapter 5.

This is where things start to get interesting. Once a company has some reports, we need to work through all the issues to extract actionable insights. We will cover all of these in Chapters 6 to 9.

---

[3] "Debate Lesson." Blog Post, Alan Weiss, https://alanweiss.com/debate-lesson/ (accessed on August 1, 2019).

Finally, we can work on establishing a data-driven culture that isn't just words on a wall. We will cover this in Chapter 10.

The great thing about the DAL model is that it allows companies to be in-between stages. You may have an ok strategy but a great implementation or solid reporting but limited insights. This represents a reality where most companies are doing fine in some areas and could do better in others.

In this book, my goal is to help you get better at every stage while still focusing on driving meaningful changes in your business. That being said, we will need to walk before running and in some cases, we'll have to crawl.

Walk before You Run (or Crawl)

We live in a culture of instant gratification that has changed how we think about the world. This isn't just something that is happening to teenagers but everyone has had their expectations warped.

Let me give you an example from my life. I live in Vancouver, Canada, where until recently (early 2020), we didn't have Uber or Lyft. To catch a cab, you either had to hail one from the street or call for one. The first option is not something I'm personally familiar with and feels inefficient. The second option could easily take upwards of 30 minutes before a taxi arrived at your house.

Fast forward to today, we now have a third option: book an Uber or Lyft. The first few times were great but when the novelty wore off, I noticed that I would get frustrated if I had to wait more than five minutes for the Uber/Lyft. My expectations on how quickly taxis should arrive changed within days of the arrival of Uber and Lyft.

This is why I understand when executives feel frustrated with their lack of data and lack of progress in this area. Why can't we just solve this problem and move on?

Unfortunately, moving groups of people in a specific direction takes time. Getting people on board, shifting priorities, and making technical changes are all time consuming. Data also suffers from a fourth limitation which is the time it takes to actually collect it.

Most of my clients have tried to get to the future but are making little progress. You may be running fast but if you're doing that on a treadmill, you won't go anywhere. This is where the DAL comes in handy. It gives us a simple map to understand what we need to tackle next and what we can worry about later.

We also need to think about rebuilding the trust in data and its purpose. I find that some of my clients have burned bridges trying to get data strategies implemented. A common example is engineering teams who have been asked repeatedly to implement tools just to see those efforts go to waste. They eventually become skeptical of any data initiatives and this is something that needs to be worked through.

That being said, companies can make great progress in 30 days or less especially if you're organized and tackle things in the right order. Before you ever ask any of your engineers to write code, you'll have a solid plan that has been thought out and tested for weaknesses. That is our goal in this book and one that we can work together on.

Case Studies of Successful Data-Driven Organizations

To understand where we are going, we need to look at those who are already there. I want to walk you through three case studies of how companies have used to drive growth within their business.

Even though these businesses might have significantly more resources than you, remember that technical limitations are rarely the main issue and instead they have to deal with the human problems at a larger scale than yourself.

One of my favorite companies is Spotify, the music app service. I use their product every day; I'm a paying user and a huge proponent of it. They also happen to have one of the best data programs in the industry.[4] One of the key aspects of the product is their curated playlists which Spo-

---

[4] "The Amazing Ways Spotify Uses Big Data, AI And Machine Learning To Drive Business Success." *Technology News, Forbes,* https://forbes.com/sites/bernard-marr/2017/10/30/the-amazing-ways-spotify-uses-big-data-ai-and-machine-learning-to-drive-business-success/#5a0844994bd2 (accessed on October 30, 2017).

tify generates automatically based on popular songs. You have playlists of the most popular Beatles songs, relevant workout songs, and songs to put you to sleep.

Spotify uses its usage data to show every user relevant new playlists that were built to their tastes. They also release this data to artists so they can see what users are listening to and how they are discovering their music. They also have their own internal framework for how to use data to make better decisions which they call DIBB (Data-Insight-Belief-Bet).[5] We'll be talking more about these kinds of frameworks in Chapter 7.

Another great case study is Airbnb, the marketplace for finding and booking rooms. They have used data extensively to improve the booking process, making it easier for hosts to accept bookings and even in how they built their data science team to be gender balanced.[6]

They have also contributed quite a few projects to the open source world including Apache Superset, Omniduct, and Aersolve. Their data teams share their learnings on a regular basis and they have found practical ways of using machine learning to make the experience better for their users.

Data isn't just something for multibillion dollar companies like Spotify and Airbnb. Companies of all sizes can take advantage of the changes in technology and find the insights they need to grow. One of my clients, Paymark, is an example of how smaller companies can use data as a competitive advantage.

Paymark is a New Zealand-based payments provider. They are able to use data to improve their product suite such as their Insights product which provides metrics and statistics to their merchants. Based on product data, the Paymark launched a redesign of their product which simplified the overall experience for their customers.

Paymark is also able to use data to provide context to real-world situations. After the Covid-19 virus started spreading to New Zealand, they were able

---

[5] "Spotify Rhythm—how we get aligned (slides from my talk at Agile Sverige)." Blog Post, *Crisp*, https://blog.crisp.se/2016/06/08/henrikkniberg/spotify-rhythm (accessed on June 8, 2016).

[6] "How Airbnb Uses Data Science to Improve Their Product and Marketing." Blog Post, *Neil Patel*, https://neilpatel.com/blog/how-airbnb-uses-data-science/ (accessed on January 23, 2020).

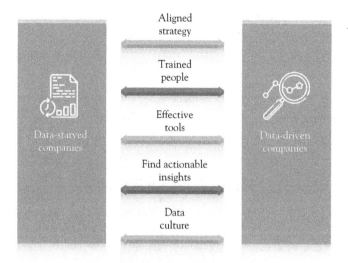

Figure 1.2 Data Proficiency Level (DPL) from Data Starved to Data Driven

to show how the virus was affecting spending patterns across the country.[7] Download more successful case studies by visiting datamiragebook.com.

Let's now look at where your company ranks when it comes to data. I created a short assessment called DPL (Data Proficiency Level) to help companies understand their strengths and weaknesses. Companies are usually strong in a few areas and could use some help in others. Figure 1.2 shows what DPL looks like.

You want to rank your company (or team) on a scale of 1 to 10 across the following categories:

- **Aligned Strategy:** Is your team and people on the same page when it comes to your strategy?
- **Trained People:** Are the people in your team fully trained on your data, tools, and processes?
- **Effective Tools:** How effective are your current technology choices?

---

[7] "Virus spreads to spending patterns." *Press Release*, Paymark, https://img.scoop. co.nz/media/pdfs/2003/Paymark__Monthly_Release_Mar20_FINAL_1.docx (accessed on March 3, 2020).

- **Find Actionable Insights:** How long does it take to find insights and build reports with your data?
- **Data Culture:** Does your company use data on a regular basis?

It doesn't matter where your company is right now when it comes to data. I'll help you close the gap and tackle the biggest challenges that you are facing and will come across as your company grows.

Hiring Unicorn Talent

We can't begin to talk about strategy without understanding the role people will play in that plan. Whether you call them A-players, unicorn talent, or something else, adding the right people to the bus is important and one of the biggest concerns for my clients.

As a side note, I'm fascinated by how the word "unicorn" has become commonplace in our world. Unicorns are supposed to be something that kids think about; instead, I hear it used all the time in boardrooms.

Clients are trying to find and hire the best "unicorn" talent. These are typically people who have a strong grasp of business (marketing, sales, etc.) but are also technically trained so they are able to code or read code.

As you can imagine, these people aren't common. People tend to naturally organize themselves around interests, and business and engineering aren't a natural overlap. The education system also hasn't historically been designed to nurture these two different skill sets. While this is changing rapidly, companies are still stuck trying to operate in an ever-increasing technical world.

For my clients, I help them tackle this in two ways: externally and internally. Externally is what most companies think about when they think about hiring: creating job descriptions, interviewing folks, and onboarding them. This could be an entire book on its own. I'll talk about the roles of people you could hire in the next chapter.

In this chapter, I want to focus on the internal option. I constantly find myself working alongside incredibly smart and driven people but they feel like they can't do certain things with data because they aren't "technical enough." What they don't realize is that they don't need a CS degree to get more value out of their data.

They simply need to learn a handful of skills that will be immediately relevant to their day-to-day work. The process of teaching these skills will be covered in Chapter 6 but here are the primary skills that every data-driven individual needs.

Basic HTML/CSS/Javascript

The first skill that every data-driven individual needs is a basic understanding of the technologies that underlie digital products. These would include HTML, CSS, and Javascript at a minimum.

This doesn't mean that these persons could work as full-time engineer but they understand how products are built at basic level and could write simple lines of code or understand code that is given to them.

This is the biggest skill gap that my clients are seeing within their teams and is a growing concern as most of the work we all do is heavily intertwined by technology. As Andreessen Horowitz, a well-known venture capitalist, said back in 2011, "software is eating the world."[8]

Human Behavior

The next skill that individuals should have is a keen understanding of human behavior. Data points can tell you a story but this story will only make sense if you understand how humans typically behave.

Let's take the chart in Figure 1.3 as an example of predictable user behavior.

We can see consistent drops in the chart which happen to correspond to Saturday and Sunday. Based on this report and an understanding of how humans worked, we could deduct that this product is primarily used during work days. If this is true, that will color any other analysis that we do because we can imagine typical persons and how they spend their work days.

---

[8] "Why Software Is Eating the World." Blog Post, A16Z, https://a16z.com/2011/08/20/why-software-is-eating-the-world/ (accessed August 20, 2011).

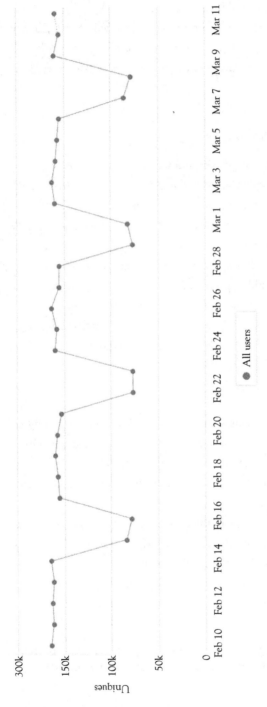

Figure 1.3 Anonymous data from a client using a tool called Amplitude[9]

[9] "Amplitude | Product Analytics for Web and Mobile." *Homepage*, Amplitude, https://amplitude.com/ (accessed on May 7, 2020).

Statistics

Next, we have statistics. This can be a dreaded topic as people get transported back to university where they spent countless hours learning what seemed like useless techniques.

From a business perspective, we don't need complex statistics most of the time. Instead, we need basic skills that will affect nearly any analysis that we do such as:

- How to properly visualize and group data
- How to average, max, and min a data
- Understand statistical significance when running experiments
- Measure the spread of the data and find outliers

If you're a full-time data analyst or data scientist, you will need to go beyond the basics and we will cover more advanced requirements in Chapter 10.

Probabilities

Another skill that all individuals should understand is the use of probabilities. This skill wasn't on my radar for a few years but it has become more important as time goes on. This skill matters because every day we are making bets on what is likely to work and most people aren't calculating the correct probabilities.

Ray Dalio, founder of Bridgewater Associates, talks about determining the expected value of any decision (or bet in our context) in his book *Principles*.[10] Let's imagine that you're deciding between two potential experiments which require similar efforts. Experiment 1 has a 50 percent probability of succeeding and a potential impact of $10,000 annually. Experiment 2 has a 20 percent probability of succeeding but a potential impact of $50,000 annually.

---

[10] "Make your decisions as expected value calculations." *Linkedin Post, Ray Dalio,* https://linkedin.com/pulse/make-your-decisions-expected-value-calculations-ray-dalio/ (accessed on October 31, 2018).

The expected value of experiment 1 is $5,000 ($10,000 × 50 percent) and experiment 2 has an expected value of $10,000 ($50,000 × 20 percent). Based on these numbers, it would make more sense to run experiment 2 as it has a higher expected value even though the probability of success is lower.

The skill of probability involves understanding these kinds of comparisons and also being able to quickly run the numbers on any set of decisions or experiments that your team is considering.

Storytelling

The final skill that all individuals should learn is the ability to tell stories. Data points and charts on their own tend to be boring. It's the story behind them that makes them interesting. If we go back to the chart under the human behavior section, it was the story of how people are using this product during work days that made it interesting. We could expand on this by explaining how users feel when they use the product or why their usage is so predictable.

Humans are wired for stories, and being able to tell a coherent story with your data is a critical skill. If you have ever been stuck in a boring meeting where someone is sharing numbers and the torture seems to go on forever, it was likely due to the lack of stories. We don't care about numbers despite how "good" they might be. We care about the human story behind them.

As you can imagine, finding individuals that have all these skills will be extremely rare but that's not the point. Instead, you can focus on teaching these skills through training and coaching. This is the approach that my clients have used with great success and without having to go to the end of the earth to find the "perfect" employee.

Do Job Titles Matter?

Since we are talking about hiring people, we also need to briefly touch upon job titles. It seems that job titles are always changing in our industry and I constantly find myself confused as to what someone actually does. We don't just have marketers but we have growth marketers or growth hackers or growth ninjas. As a side note, I have no idea how "ninja" became a potential job title.

That being said, how much do titles matter? Do you need the latest version or should you stick with more traditional values? The answer: it depends.

Based on my experience, having modern titles tends to attract the right candidates especially if you're hiring for something that is relatively new. Marketers with a more technical background and with experience working with digital products will likely know what "growth marketer" or "demand generation specialist" means.

The caveat is that you will need to gauge how your local market thinks about titles. I find that my clients in San Francisco can be quite specific with their titles because everyone is up to date with how roles and departments are changing. My clients in other cities and countries might not be aware of these trends yet and you'll simply end up repelling potential candidates.

Conclusion

This chapter is the pre-takeoff announcement that you hear on any flight. I need us to calibrate expectations, show you why companies struggle to be data driven, and give you a glimpse into what the best companies are doing.

We also briefly talked about people and the skills that you need to look for in your team. While we won't cover how to hire in this book, we will talk about how to use training and coaching to nurture the internal unicorn talent that your organization already has.

That being said, we can move on and start designing a strategy that can survive contact with the real world. We'll talk about getting the right people onboard, choosing KPIs and much more.

Chapter Summary

- Technology is rarely the limited factor for companies who want to use data but people and psychology are.
- You can use DAL to determine in what areas your company performs well and what areas need help.
- Trust in data is important and something that needs to be repaired and maintained.
- You can hire externally or internally for "unicorn" talent but focus on the right skills.

CHAPTER 2

Designing Data Strategies for the Real World

The essence of strategy is choosing what not to do.

—Michael Porter

It seemed like the fires would never stop burning. I found myself in the middle of a project where everything was falling apart, all the time. We were missing deadlines, people were unhappy, and I was tired. This didn't make much sense to me. The work we wanted to do wasn't hard. I had done similar work before with great results. We just couldn't get things right in this project.

This is the point where you realize the value of strategy. We were lost in the middle of the forest. We couldn't see the way out because all the trees looked the same. In this project, all we could do was keep putting out the fires and hope to find a minute to breathe. Pausing can seem weird when there's chaos but sometimes it's the only sensible answer.

Strategy is one of the most talked about areas in business. The value of a good strategy is common knowledge but I still come across companies that skipped it altogether. They will "figure it out" as they go along. This sometimes works and other times, it backfires spectacularly.

I don't believe that you should spend months on strategy but give it an appropriate amount of time. In this chapter, we'll look at my process for helping companies determine a data strategy that will maximize their chances of success. The goal is insights and that's what our strategy should optimize around.

Plan Before You Execute

One of the biggest mistakes that I see with my clients is an eagerness to jump into execution and tactics right away. Almost all of my sales conversations start with "what do you think about software X?" or "how do we fix our high churn rate?"

This makes it more likely that you will choose the wrong tools, enlist the wrong people, and even fail to get any insights out of your data. This is why we will spend this chapter looking at all the planning that should be done before your team ever writes a single line of code.

I know what some of you may be thinking. "No plan survives contact with the enemy" or something along those lines. This is true but the act of planning is valuable in itself. Our plan will also take reality into account instead of trying to predict some abstract future.

That being said, the heart of my data strategies revolves around the 3Ps: People, Process, and Providers (Figure 2.1).

I organize the 3Ps into a pyramid to show the different levels of importance to each step. People are the most important because they are ones that are actually going to be using the data and the area where companies will run into the most challenges. A good portion of this book is dedicated to solving the people problems that arise when working with data.

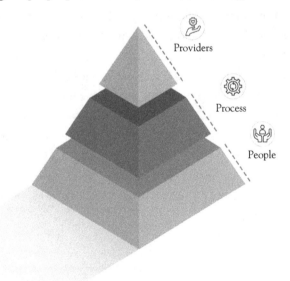

Figure 2.1 3Ps provide an outline for your data strategy

Process comes second and this looks at how your team works through your data to find relevant insights. Companies should have clear ways of sharing team data internally, best practices around core reports, and a universal language around the data.

Finally, we have Providers which encompasses software tools. This is where companies like to start but that's a mistake. It's easier than ever to find the right tools for your business and it doesn't make much sense to optimize your business around this area first. Once you figure out People and Process, choosing the right tools will be even easier.

At the end of this planning session, you will have a simple document outlining the major points and answers to these three areas. We'll then add any missing details in the upcoming chapters. See the 3Ps in action by by visting datamiragebook.com and download extra bonuses.

Let's now look at each area in detail and start fleshing out our data plan.

People

We start with People because it doesn't matter how sophisticated your tools or your processes are if your team can't use them. I also find that this is the biggest variable at my clients because they all have slightly different makeups and this affects everything in their data strategy.

Teams that are highly technical can take advantage of more advanced tools while teams that are constrained by their technical capacity need to find solutions that are user friendly. When companies get this incorrectly, they end up with tools and processes that no one can use.

The first step in our People strategy is to assess our team on a few key categories. I created an assessment called the Measuring Team Skills (MTS) for my clients, which is a quick way of understanding the makeup of your team (Figure 2.2).

I want to understand how every person ranks themselves alongside the following categories.

- **Technical Expertise:** How technical is this person?
- **Probability Thinking:** Do they understand how to think about probabilities?

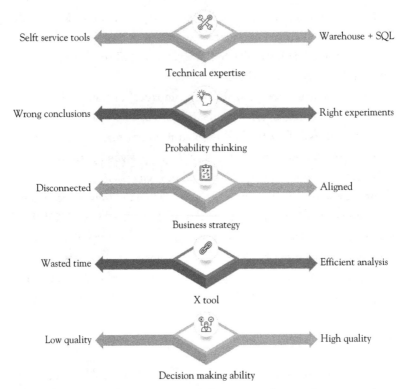

Selft service tools ← Technical expertise → Warehouse + SQL

Wrong conclusions ← Probability thinking → Right experiments

Disconnected ← Business strategy → Aligned

Wasted time ← X tool → Efficient analysis

Low quality ← Decision making ability → High quality

Figure 2.2 The MTS assessment helps you understand your team's skill makeup

- **Business Strategy:** Are they able to align their work to overall business strategy?
- **X Tools:** How comfortable do they feel with their existing tools?
- **Decision Making Ability:** What is the quality of their decisions?

Everyone will fill out a short form where they will rate themselves on each category using a scoring system of 1 to 10. I can then take all the individual scores and average them to see how the overall team scores in these areas. If I'm dealing with multiple teams, I'll average out the scores by team instead of grouping everyone together.

Once I have this data, I can start to make decisions on what tools would be a good fit and what training should I be considering for a given team. I'll show you how to use this data to inform you answers to questions under Processes and Providers.

Next, you also want to consider the following questions.

Who Is Going to Own the Data on the Business Side and the Technical Side?

Everyone can access the data but there should be a clear owner that people can reach out. Common questions will include clarifications on what is being tracked, what tools are available, and best practices for analysis.

The technical side is also important because you will need support to maintain any data tracking and implementation. It's also helpful to have a champion within the technical team who can advocate for the data. Without this support, you'll find that your tracking is constantly breaking as you release new product changes or features.

Who Do You Need to Hire?

If you're missing any key roles, this is where you want to make note of that. You may need to hire data analysts, data engineers, data scientists, or some other combination of skills. You can think of your hiring in two broad categories: who's going to implement/maintain the data and who's going to analyze it.

Choosing the right tools can help in this area especially if you have people in your team who could analyze data if it's provided to them in approachable format. However, keep in mind that this kind of analysis is limited to what a full-time data analyst or data scientist could be doing.

Whose Support Do You Need Internally?

Consider who will support you in this plan. This would include technical resources such as engineers but it might also include legal counsel to help you sort through data privacy issues, other executives and leaders, and even your own team.

Think about who could benefit from this data and who could block this strategy from proceeding forward.

At the end of this step, you will have an overview of the people that will need to be involved in this strategy and some initial ideas on what they need. Let's now look at Process and the questions you need to answer there.

Making Sense of the Different Data Roles

If you're thinking of hiring, you need to make sure that you look for the correct roles. I'll give you a brief explanation of what kind of roles you can expect in the marketplace and which one might be the fit for your company.

Data Analyst: This role is responsible for generating reports and dashboards. They may do that through BI tools like Tableau and Excel or take advantage of modern technologies like R and python. This is a great role for companies who have data in different locations and need someone to tell them "what happened." Most companies can benefit from having more data analysts.

Data Scientist: This might be one of the sexiest job titles right now but also one of the most misunderstood. They are typically focused on using data to build models. These models could help with fraud, product optimization, or something else. Their work is more long term and less day to day. It's common to come across data scientists who are actually data analysts in disguise.

Data Engineer: This role is someone who can help data get from point A to point B. They are typically a backend or full stack engineer and specialize in understanding how data is collected. They are working alongside data analysts or data scientists to give them easy access to data.

Machine Learning Engineer: This role might be blended into data engineers or data scientists. If it's a separate role, they would specialize in moving and capturing data for machine learning models. They could function as a data engineer but might have a stronger background in machine learning and statistics.

Data Architect: This role specializes in designing the overall system for collecting data. They are working alongside data engineers and data analysts/ scientists to determine what data needs to be captured. This role might be done by a data engineer in small companies and less complex systems.

Business Analyst: This role is similar to data analysts but business analysts tend to be more business-focused. They could serve a bridge between technical roles and business roles. In the past, they have been limited in their technical skills but this is changing quickly.

Data and Analytics Manager: This role is in charge of managing analytics teams. They would get any other data roles and get what they need from other teams and resources. This would only be needed once the data team is of sufficient size. If the team is small, data roles will fall under other teams.

When my clients are starting to hire, we typically look toward data analysts first as they can help with day-to-day reporting. Engineering teams can typically manage the initial work but we may also start looking for a data engineer once complexity starts to increase. Finally, we would look for data scientists and similar roles once the company is ready to undertake significant machine learning work.

Process

Process is something that I didn't use to pay much attention to until I started to run into the problem of having too much data. Some of my clients started creating dashboards and reports left and right (which was great) but then they started duplicating their efforts. Someone would analyze the marketing performance and three weeks later, someone else would do the same.

I then started to think about how companies should approach the process of analyzing and sharing data. In this section, you can answer the following questions:

How Are We Going to Share and Consume Data?

This starts to touch into the world of tools but you can start to think about how people want to consume and share data. Some people will want to jump right into the raw data and play with it while others simply want summaries of what is going on.

Your data plan needs to address these different needs and take into account the technical capacity of your team (refer back to the MTS assessment). Think about how people could talk about data in a collaborative way using tools like Slack or Microsoft Teams.

Where Are We Going to Store Best Practices and Documentation?

As your team gets familiar with the data, you'll start to develop best practices including definitions for your most important KPIs (key performance indicators) and fundamental reports. Store all of this information in a centralized location where everyone can access it and suggest improvements.

In particular, capture the following best practices:

- What are the most important KPIs to your business and how do you define them?
- What are the most important reports and are there any specific considerations to understand before using them?
- What tools and data are available right now?

What Issues or Challenges Are We Going to Run Into?

Finally, we can spend some time thinking about what issues or challenges you might encounter. This can include issues such as data accuracy, pushback from other teams, lack of centralized best practices, and issues in training. We will cover many of these issues in upcoming chapters and you'll have a chance to revisit them very soon.

Now that you have an idea of how your company will manage and analyze data, we move on to Providers, everyone's favorite topic.

Providers

This might be the whole reason why you bought this book. You want to know the best tools for doing X and how software can make things easier for you. Once we do the upfront work in People and Process, we can reward ourselves by talking about tools.

This is such a large portion of the data plan that I dedicated the entirety of Chapter 3 to the tool selection process. In that chapter, we'll look at the different categories that you need be aware of, how to handle privacy, and much more.

I would suggest that you wait a few minutes before jumping straight there as we'll continue talking about KPIs, the most challenges you will face, and how to plan in the future in the remainder of this chapter.

For now, remember that providers (or tools) are meant to support your team. They can be used to close the gaps that you may be seeing and they could help optimize your limited resources. They are not a panacea that will solve all your problems.

KPIs for the Modern World

KPI might be one of the most used words in the business world. Everyone wants to know the current performance on the KPIs or how the KPIs are changing.

Let's start by looking at a few principles behind choosing the best KPIs for your business. Every company or industry will look at different things but the principles behind them tend to be universal.

How to Choose KPIs

When looking at your KPIs, we need to start by dividing them into leading and lagging indicators. Leading indicators help you understand what will happen and tend to be more helpful in short-term analysis. If we look at digital advertising, leading indicators would be things like the click-through rate, cost per click, and the conversion rate of the landing page.

Lagging indicators help you understand what happened and tend to be aligned with long-term analysis (Figure 2.3). In your digital advertising example, lagging indicators would be number of conversions, revenue, and profit. Some indicators could be leading or lagging depending on how you define and track them.

Neither category is better than the other but you want to have a healthy balance of both. This is especially helpful for industries with long cycles such as enterprise software businesses with their long sales cycles or manufacturing with their long production cycles.

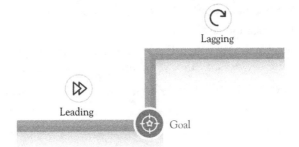

Figure 2.3 Leading versus lagging indicators

If you feel like you're flying blind in your business, you're likely missing leading indicators and if you feel like you don't understand what has worked so far, then you're likely missing lagging indicators.

After this split, consider the difference between quantitative and qualitative KPIs. I love numbers but they can only tell part of the story. The qualitative story can be extremely rich and helpful and most companies should be tracking more of it.

More companies should be diving deeper into their qualitative data. You can use the 2 × 2 axis chart to understand how missing qualitative data can give you an incomplete picture into your business (Figure 2.4).

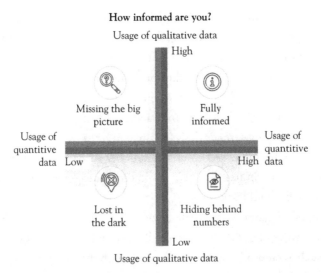

Figure 2.4 How informed are you?

The best companies use both types of data to be "Fully Informed." You could easily hide behind your KPIs by only using quantitative data and you could miss the big picture by only looking at qualitative data.

Finally, if you're ever unsure of what to track, simply look toward other companies in your industry. KPI is not the place for innovation and most companies should be tracking roughly the same things that matter within their industry. Getting creative with your KPIs and their definitions can come back and bite you in the ass as you try to raise funding, get acquired, or go public.

Incentives behind KPIs

One of my favorite ideas behind KPIs is around the incentives they create. I once worked with a company in the tourism industry and one of their KPIs for their marketing campaigns was pageviews.

As a result, all of their advertising partners optimize their campaigns and spending around generating pageviews. There is nothing wrong with pageviews but be sure that this is the behavior that you're actually interested in. Don't assume that more pageviews will result in more contact form requests. Instead, optimize around contact form requests if that is your end goal.

Every KPI has incentives and people (and teams) will do their best to optimize around them. There is nothing malicious here, just basic human behavior. If you determine that you would like to optimize around users logging in to your product and nothing more, then people will figure out the best ways to get users to log in. You might end up seeing dog and cat pictures even if they have nothing to do with your product.

Explaining Them to Your Teams

Finally, have clear definitions for what KPIs mean in your business. I'm always surprised when I first start working with companies and I ask them about their most important KPIs. Almost always, I get different definitions from different teams.

This ties back into what we talked about in the Process section where you can have a central place where you can store best practices and basic information about your data. If you're starting to talk about the cost to acquire a customer, active users, or retained users, everyone should know exactly what you're referring to.

Expect the Unexpected

As we get into the nitty gritty of implementation, I want to point out the three major challenges that will face over the next 12 months. We'll be diving into specifics in future chapters but I want you to start thinking about them.

Pushback from Other Teams

The first challenge will be an internal pushback from other teams. This might come from the engineering team who are unable or unwilling to give you the necessary implementation time. You might also get pushback from the legal/compliance team who are concerned about where data will be stored and shared.

Regardless of where the pushback comes from, we need to understand the true issues and deal with them. We'll work with all of these teams to find common ground and make compromises on our data plan.

Choosing the Wrong Tools

The second challenge is choosing the wrong tools for your team and company. This is happening less over time but it's still something we should be concerned about. We'll do our best to choose the best tools based on what our company needs and what our people can do but there's guaranteed that everything will work.

All of the upfront work that I'm getting you to go through is designed to minimize the chance of making the wrong choices at the software level which typically means investing significant engineering time or signing six-figure licensing deals.

Lack of Interest or Trust in Data

The third and final challenge will revolve around getting your team to use and trust the data. The premise of this book is that most of the work is about dealing with this challenge and I dedicated multiple chapters to dealing with it. People are complicated making them the hardest variable to understand. Software and process are easier by comparison.

Think about these three challenges and how they will apply to your company. You can start to lay the foundation by getting the right people onboard and trying to predict where you will have issues.

Now that we covered how to start building your data plan, we can look at the final element: Providers or Tools.

Chapter Summary

- A good data plan will help you see the trees from the forest.
- Companies like to start with tools but instead start with your people and your processes.
- People will be the biggest variable at your company and where you will run into the most challenges.
- Process is an understated area of data strategy but will come in handy when you're starting to analyze your data.
- Providers (or tools) are meant to support your organization. We will dedicate Chapter 3 to selecting tools.

CHAPTER 3

How to Avoid Drowning in Tool Hell and Safeguarding Your Data

Instead of freaking out about these constraints, embrace them. Let them guide you. Constraints drive innovation and force focus. Instead of trying to remove them, use them to your advantage.
—37Signals, *Getting Real: The Smarter, Faster, Easier Way to Build a Web Application*

When I meet with a new company, I like to play a game. I try to predict what issues that company will share with me and how they came to be to their current situation.

My predictions are pretty close to the actual truth in most cases. I sometimes tell clients my predictions (or "guesses") and some are taken aback at my seemingly uncanny ability to read their minds.

In reality, I have seen situations like these hundreds of times so it's really a matter of being able to connect the dots. When it comes to choosing software tools, there are a few pitfalls that everyone needs to avoid.

Let me paint you a picture of how this plays out with most of my clients and how this might eventually apply to your situation.

The management team of a company decides that they are finally committed to being data driven. This is what will help them crush their annual goals, beat their competitors, and deliver a better experience to their customers.

They spend an hour talking about the future and all the things they will now be able to do. The excitement in the room is electrifying. They know that any good project requires someone to take the lead so they assign a person to make all this happen. Whatever they need from other teams, they got it.

This person leaves the meeting feeling excited and slightly apprehensive. Will it be an easy task? Can they do it on their own? Who else do they need to get involved?

The first item on their plate is to research software tools and put together a list of these together to the best ones for their company. How hard can this be?

Thirty minutes into their research, this person realizes that choosing the "best" software tools is a massive project. There are so many questions such as:

- How can you compare tools with similar functionality?
- How much involvement will be needed from the engineering team?
- Are they going to outgrow a tool in 12 months?
- Should they be worried about vendor lock in?
- Will this fit into the company's data privacy policies?

This initially simple project is quickly turning complex. Worst of all, it's just one step of a very long process involving actually implementing the tools, building reports, extracting insights from them, and using those insights to make better decisions.

I'm here to help you sort through the noise of software vendor tools and get you closer to what you actually want: actionable insights that lead to dramatic improvements to your business.

You Need Questions Answered, Not Tools

Whenever clients ask me about tools, I tell them that we shouldn't start the conversation there. Instead, we need to focus on what questions they would like to answer.

This helps them relax because companies tend to have a good grasp of what questions they already have. How they answer those questions is where tools come in.

I like to group data questions into general categories and work with companies to figure out which categories are currently most important to them.

Over time, a company will be able to answer all of these categories, but we need insights today and can't wait until we have all the data possible. Prioritizing at this stage will also help us cut down the implementation time needed to get up and running.

Here is a list of the most popular categories to think about:

1. What is the performance of our marketing dollars?
2. What are the common behaviors of our best users?
3. How do we best communicate with our users?
4. What do our users think about our products or services?
5. How do we easily visualize data from multiple sources?
6. How can we manage data ingestion and privacy?
7. How do we move data from point A to point B?
8. How do we improve our existing sales processes?
9. How do we easily track key financial ratios and metrics?
10. What's the best way to detect and combat fraud?
11. How do we reduce errors and technical issues in our operations?
12. What's the best way to increase customer satisfaction?
13. How do I keep my management team informed?

I find that companies can typically focus on one to two categories at a time without feeling overwhelmed or spending months in implementation. Let me break down each category in detail and show you some common tools to seed your research efforts.

What Is the Performance of Our Marketing Dollars?

In this category, we are focused on understanding the impact of our marketing campaigns and channels. This is commonly referred to as marketing attribution, which can take place across web and mobile channels.

The world of attribution can be complex and quite technical, but you can start with the basics and layer on more advanced techniques over time.

At the most basic level, we want to see a report that breaks down our campaigns and gives us an ROI calculation of our spending. This will look something like in Figure 3.1.

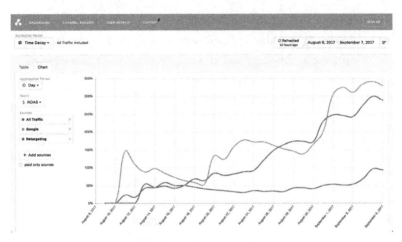

Figure 3.1 A marketing attribution report from AttributionApp[1]

We are interested in knowing how many users or customers a campaign/channel drove, how much that campaign/channel cost, and how much revenue (or some other conversion like sign-ups) we got out of it.

As mentioned above, the attribution location is important and will determine what tools you will need. Here is a breakdown of where attribution can happen:

1. Websites on desktops or mobile devices, for example, e-commerce purchases, sign-ups for web apps, pageviews, videos watched
2. Mobile apps on iOS or Android, for example, app installs, in-app purchases, mobile conversions
3. Offline, for example, retail purchases, event attendance

Attributing conversions on websites is easier than mobile apps which is easier than offline activities. This complexity comes down to how people can be tracked across digital versus offline channels.

---

[1] "Home—Attribution." *Homepage, AttributionApp*, https://attributionapp.com/ (accessed on April 1, 2020).

This book isn't meant to be a comprehensive look at tracking methods, but you can dig deeper into browser cookies, fingerprint methods, device IDs, and people-based attribution for more information.

Let's now look at specific tools for tackling each of the three attribution locations listed earlier.

Web Attribution

The gold standard in this space is Google Analytics (GA). The free version of GA is installed on millions of websites and is known by almost all companies.

Their attribution report looks like in Figure 3.2.

This requires some setup in terms of getting GA on your website and tracking the relevant conversions, but it's still one of the easiest ways to start attributing your web traffic. Spending per channel isn't typically available here, so you will need to export this data and combine it with your spending to get a clear ROI.

There are also alternatives to GA such as Matomo (open source solution) and Piwik Pro, which have been built to be very similar to how GA thinks about data.

GA also offers an enterprise version called Google Analytics 360 which expands on all the basic functionality. This offering starts at $100,000+ per year.

Mobile App Attribution

Mobile app attribution is harder than web attribution because users have to go through the Apple Store or the Play Store to download your app. This intermediate step acts as a "black hole" where data can be lost.

Both Apple and Google provide some basic attribution but it's typically quite limited. Instead, you can use tools like Appsflyer and Branch. io which are meant to help shine a light on this black hole.

Their attribution reports for these tools look like in Figure 3.3.

These tools will build a global database of user identifiers, which you can then access to be able to link user activity before people go through the app store and after they install your app. From your perspective, this

Medium	Acquisition			Behavior			Conversions Goal 1: Signup: Completed		
	Sessions ?	% New sessions ?	New users ?	Bounce rate ?	Pages/ session ?	Avg. session duration ?	Signup: Completed (Goal 1 conversion rate) ?	Signup: Completed (Goal 1 completions) ?	Signup: Completed (Goal 1 value) ?
	20,296 % of Total: 100.00% (20,296)	54.21% Avg for view: 54.17% (0.08%)	11,003 % of Total: 100.08% (10,994)	57.31% avg for View: 57.31% (0.00%)	2.02 Avg View: 2.02 (0.00%)	00:02:19 Avg for View: 00:02:19 (0.00%)	0.73% Avg for View: 0.73% (0.00%)	149 % of Total: 100.00% (149)	$89,400.00 % of Total: 100.00% ($89,400.00)
1. (none)	10,867 (53.54%)	62.39%	6,780 (61.62%)	56.43%	1.94	00:02:07	0.60%	65 (43.62%)	$39,000.00 (43.62%)
2. organic	4,736 (23.33%)	41.72%	1,976 (17.96%)	55.49%	2.17	00:02:52	0.70%	33 (22.15%)	$19,800.00 (22.15%)
3. referral	2,149 (10.59%)	50.81%	1,092 (9.92%)	56.03%	2.26	00:02:31	1.44%	31 (20.81%)	$18,600.00 (20.81%)
4. cpc	1,611 (7.94%)	50.65%	816 (7.42%)	65.92%	1.86	00:01:57	0.81%	13 (8.72%)	$7,800.00 (8.72%)
5. email	713 (3.51%)	33.66%	240 (2.18%)	64.66%	1.91	00:02:09	0.84%	6 (4.03%)	$3,600.00 (4.03%)
6. social_media	74 (0.36%)	27.03%	20 (0.18%)	71.62%	1.73	00:02:10	0.00%	0 (0.00%)	$0.00 (0.00%)
7. social_media_pd	59 (0.29%)	79.66%	47 (0.43%)	69.49%	1.53	00:01:20	0.00%	0 (0.00%)	$0.00 (0.00%)
8. listing	35 (0.17%)	80.00%	28 (0.25%)	54.29%	2.23	00:02:19	0.00%	0 (0.00%)	$0.00 (0.00%)
9. product	11 (0.05%)	36.36%	4 (0.04%)	72.73%	1.36	00:03:02	0.00%	0 (0.00%)	$0.00 (0.00%)
10. uc-in-app	10 (0.05%)	0.00%	0 (0.00%)	40.00%	2.70	00:02:05	10.00%	1 (0.67%)	$600.00 (0.67%)

Figure 3.2 An attribution report from Google Analytics[2]

---

[2] "Analytics Tools and Solutions for Your Business - Google Analytics." *Homepage, Google Analytics*, https://marketingplatform.google.com/about/analytics/ (accessed on February 1, 2020).

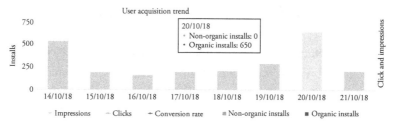

Figure 3.3 A mobile attribution report from Appsflyer³

can seem like magic but they do a lot of heavy lifting to get an estimated attribution count.

Other tools in this space include Kochava and Adjust which offer similar functionality. Look for companies with proprietary attribution models, deep linking capabilities, and other specific features that might be relevant to your app.

Offline Attribution

Offline attribution is the hardest form of attribution because you won't always have a digital method of identifying users. Instead you have to rely on "old-school" methods for connecting your spending to conversions.

Tools like Near are quite new in this space but aim to connect offline activity to a digital profile. You'll need to rely on data such as foot traffic and location, personal data such as names or e-mails, and credit card data.

Attribution Models

Beyond the three attribution locations, you also need to think about which attribution model makes sense for your business. An attribution model is a way of determining which channel or touchpoint should get credit for a conversion.

A typical customer for your business might go through multiple channels or campaigns before they actually convert. For example, they might see an ad on Facebook, search for your business through the Google

---

³ "AppsFlyer | Attribution Data You Can Trust." *Homepage, Appsflyer*, https://appsflyer.com/ (accessed January 1, 2020).

search engine, and finally visit your website directly from a bookmark (direct channel).

Most attribution tools will default to a Last Touch model which means the bookmark visit will get 100 percent of credit in our example earlier. You could also use a First Touch model which means that the Facebook ad gets 100 percent of the credit.

From there, you could explore other models such as linear, which means all three channels split the credit (33 percent each), or time decay, which provides a higher value to the earlier channels (e.g., Facebook ad) and decreases (or decays) as time goes on. This is referred to as Multi Touch attribution where you're trying to understand how each channel is playing a role in the conversion.

Last Touch and First Touch are great for companies who are just starting out while Multi Touch models require a significant investment in your analytics capabilities. A common mistake that I see is companies that try to run Multi Touch models with very little data and almost no analytics expertise.

Start with the basics and build up to more advanced techniques. Even imperfect models like Last Touch and First Touch can point you in the right direction for growth.

What Are the Common Behaviors of Our Best Users?

In this category, we are interested in understanding how our best users behave and how to acquire or create more of these users. This is typically well suited to more complex products such as web or mobile apps but there are always user behaviors across all businesses.

We can think about this category in three major buckets: new users, customers, and power users.

New users are those who have only just signed up for your product or visited your website. What should they do (in terms of actions) to get closer to becoming a customer?

Customers are those who are actually using and paying for your product. Once they become customers, we are trying to determine how to get them to upgrade to higher value services or become power users.

Power users are those who love your product. For this group, we are trying to figure out how to make them evangelists for your product.

Common tools in this category include Mixpanel, Amplitude, and Heap Analytics. These tools are event driven, which means you send them events and event properties that represent users' actions. We talked about events in Chapter 2 and how to properly define them.

Here are some of the reports you will be using this category.

Funnels

This report shows a series of steps and the drop-off among them for our users. This is applicable to check out funnels for e-commerce stores, onboarding flows for apps, or part of your product where users should be taking concrete steps (Figure 3.4).

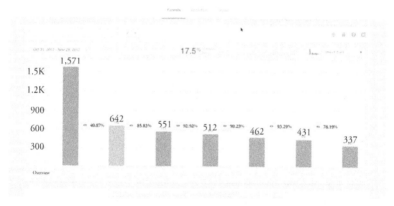

Figure 3.4 Funnel report in Mixpanel[4]

Cohort Analysis

This report groups your users into cohorts (or groups) and makes it easier to analyze their behavior over time. Using cohorts is effective because we isolate the impact of product changes or different marketing campaigns. We can use cohorts to understand long-term retention or customer value (Figure 3.5).

---

[4] "Product and User Behavioral Analytics for Mobile, Web, and More | Mixpanel." *Homepage*, Mixpanel, last modified February 13, 2020, https://mixpanel.com/

Date	People	The number of months later your users were retained									
		< 1 mth	1	2	3	4	5	6	7	8	9
Jul 1, 2017	28,341	88.22%	31.31%	25.07%	21.56%	18.93%	16.61%	14.96%	13.55%	12.54%	11.75%
Aug 1, 2017	28,368	88.73%	31.51%	26.04%	22.42%	19.92%	17.75%	16.01%	14.88%	14.02%	12.67%
Sep 1, 2017	22,176	85.00%	39.05%	32.59%	28.58%	25.07%	22.86%	21.09%	19.68%	18.15%	16.62%
Oct 1, 2017	18,378	83.61%	46.84%	39.17%	34.64%	31.21%	28.68%	26.75%	34.37%	22.45%	13.05%
Nov 1, 2017	17,535	84.47%	48.21%	41.83%	37.11%	34.07%	31.33%	28.72%	26.55%	15.47%	
Dec 1, 2017	18,264	84.94%	46.82%	40.70%	36.86%	34.25%	31.03%	28.42%	16.89%		
Jan 1, 2017	18,500	84.35%	47.51%	41.42%	38.42%	34.51%	31.54%	19.11%			
Feb 1, 2018	16,430	84.38%	51.98%	46.21%	41.80%	38.08%	23.34%				
Mar 1, 2018	16,956	84.71%	53.45%	46.97%	41.92%	27.07%					
Apr 1, 2018	17,670	84.44%	51.65%	45.56%	29.33%						
May 1, 2018	17,322	84.51%	52.32%	34.03%							
Jun 1, 2018	16,875	84.78%	39.60%								
Jul 1, 2018	15,280	80.92%									

Figure 3.5 Cohort analysis in Mixpanel[5]

---

[5] "Product and User Behavioral Analytics for Mobile, Web, and More | Mixpanel." *Homepage*, Mixpanel, https://mixpanel.com/ (accessed on February 13, 2020).

Figure 3.6 Event segmentation in Amplitude[6]

Event Segmentation

This report will allow you to segment or slice any of your events. We can see the total event counts, sum of different property values, or other calculations. This functionality is "simple" but we can answer a lot of questions around behavior and long-term trends by using a report like in Figure 3.6.

How Do We Best Communicate with Our Customers?

In this category, we need to figure out the best way to communicate with our customers. You might instantly think about e-mail but that's just the beginning. We could also communicate through SMS, in-app messages, push notifications, and physical mail.

Look at the tools that can offer multiple channels or the ability to integrate into different channels. Common options include Iterable, Marketo, Salesforce Marketing Cloud, and Autopilot.

Most companies start with e-mail messages that guide users through your product, but you can eventually expand on this in a couple of ways.

First, you can use different channels depending on your call to action. If you want users to open your app, this message might be better suited as a push notification.

---

[6] "Amplitude | Product Analytics for Web and Mobile." *Homepage*, Amplitude, https://amplitude.com/ (accessed on May 7, 2020).

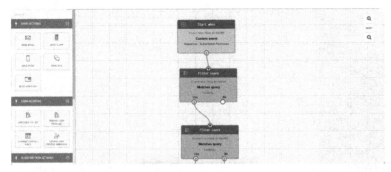

Figure 3.7 Workflow design in Iterable[7]

Second, you can trigger messages based on user behaviors. If the user signed up but didn't upload a photo, you can send a message talking about this. This becomes a series of branches where each message is highly relevant to each user (Figure 3.7).

What Do Our Users Think about Our Products or Services?

In this category, we are interested in collecting qualitative data about our products and customers. Think about surveys, NPS scores, and other reports like heatmaps or session recordings (Figure 3.8).

You can look at tools like SurveyMonkey, Hotjar, and FullStory for collecting all of this data.

The primary thing I tell my clients is that they should be thinking about how to automate the collection of this data. Instead of manually sending an NPS survey every month, design a workflow that can be automatically based on certain user behaviors or criteria.

This automation will save your team time but, more importantly, add consistency to your data efforts—a major issue with which teams often struggle.

How Do We Easily Visualize Data from Multiple Sources?

In this category, we are interested in figuring out how to combine data from multiple sources into one single dashboard or report. A common

[7] "Growth Marketing Platform for Cross-Channel Customer Engagement - Iterable." *Homepage, Iterable,* (accessed on February 4, 2020) https://iterable.com/

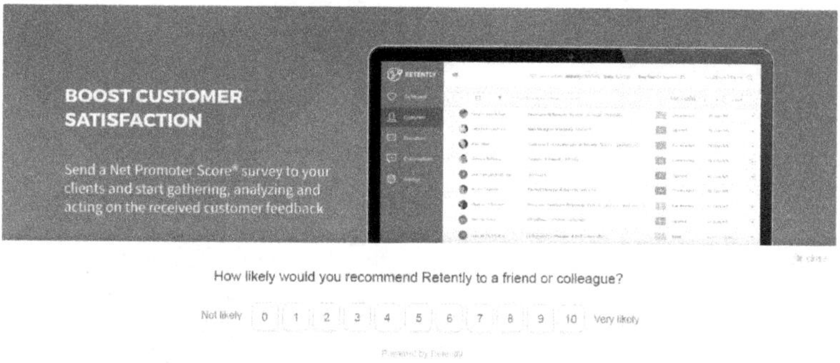

How likely would you recommend Retently to a friend or colleague?

Not likely   0   1   2   3   4   5   6   7   8   9   10   Very likely

Figure 3.8 NPS survey in a website[8]

use case is combining conversion data and cost data into a unified attribution report with ROI.

The conversion data might come from GA while the cost data comes from Facebook Ads and Google Ads. In the beginning, you might do this manually through Excel or Google Sheets but you can eventually automate this process.

Tools like Domo, Tableau, and Databox are solving this problem. Look at what data sources they support and how easy it is to run Excel-like calculations to build your reports (Figure 3.9).

For data analysts, you can look at Mode and Chartio, which require SQL knowledge and a data warehouse. This route tends to be more flexible but you need a certain level of technical expertise to pull it off.

How Can We Manage Data Ingestion and Privacy?

In this category, we need to figure out the best way to collect data and protect it. Regulations like GDPR (which we'll talk about in more detail later) are forcing companies to streamline how data gets collected and stored.

Tools like Segment.com and mParticle function as CDPs and ETLs, where you can collect data from different sources like websites, apps, and backend servers, then send them to different tools like Mixpanel, Amplitude, and AWS Redshift (data warehouses; Figure 3.10).

---

[8] "Measure and improve customer satisfaction using NPS and CSAT surveys." *Homepage, Retently*, https://retently.com/ (accessed February 1, 2020).

Figure 3.9 A dashboard example from Domo[9]

They can also simplify your implementation efforts by abstracting and normalizing your data. Moreover, they build functionality around GDPR and data privacy.

Think about centralizing how your data is collected so you have a good idea of what data you collect, where it's being sent, and how to manage it.

How Do We Move Data from Point A to Point B?

It's quite common to end up with data stuck in silos. You want to get this data into a central location like a data warehouse or data lake and this is where ETLs come in. ETL, which stands for Extract, Transform, Load, is how you get data from point A to point B.

You would use ETLs to extract your data out of a tool like Salesforce and move it to a data warehouse. From there you can visualize using the tools we mentioned in an earlier chapter. When it comes to ETLs, you're looking for compatibility with your existing tools, pricing that fits your budget, and ease of use. The better your ETL scores on this, the easier your life will be. Players like Stitch (Figure 3.11), Fivetran, and Matilion are all examples of ETL tools that you can explore.

---

[9] "BI Leverage, At Cloud Scale, In Record Time | Domo." *Homepage, Domo*, https://domo.com/ (accessed on June 26, 2020).

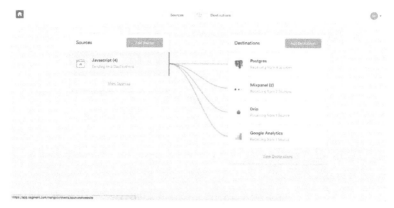

Figure 3.10 Data ingestion through Segment.com[10]

How Do We Improve Our Existing Sales Processes?

Sales processes are one of those areas ripe for improvements. In my experience, companies tend to design them once and then let run as long as they are "good enough." In this category, we need to start by accurately tracking how our customers engage with your sales teams. To do this, you will need a CRM where all reps can enter their activity.

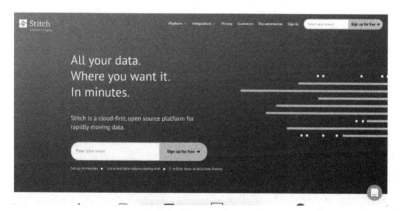

Figure 3.11 Stitch ETL homepage[11]

---

[10] "Segment | Customer Data Platform (CDP)." *Homepage, Segment,* https:// segment.com/ (accessed on January 1, 2020).

[11] "Stitch: Simple, extensible ETL built for data teams." *Homepage, Stitch,* https://stitchdata.com/ (accessed on January 1, 2020).

CRMs are quite common and there is no lack of options here. Salesforce provides a massive ecosystem (Figure 3.12), while smaller companies like Pipedrive, Zoho CRM, and Hubspot provide more lightweight alternatives.

Regardless of the option that you choose, you need to set up the following tracking:

- Unifying customers under one account or company especially if you're dealing with multiple people at the same company
- A funnel where prospects are taken through different stages
- Capturing notes, e-mails, calls, and other touchpoints with the prospect
- Dealing with information such as value, time to close, and the source of the deal

In Chapter 8, we look at how we can improve any process using this information but for now, focus on making it easy for sales reps to track their work and keeping the data clean.

Figure 3.12 Salesforce CRM[12]

---

[12] "The World's #1 CRM Software: Customer Relationship Management." *Homepage, Salesforce,* https://salesforce.com/ca/crm/ (accessed on January 1, 2020).

Figure 3.13 Quickbooks accounting software[13]

How Do We Easily Track Key Financial Ratios and Metrics?

In this category, we want to track the financial performance of your company. All companies function in the same three fundamental reports: income statement, balance sheet, and cash flow statements. You will likely also have specific ratios relevant to your business and industry.

The primary choice you need to make is on accounting software. You have options like Netsuite, Quickbooks (Figure 3.13), and Xero. Besides the core accounting reports mentioned above, you need to also consider if you need extra functionality like invoicing, expense tracking, and time tracking.

Your accounting software will output the latest version of the three fundamental reports at any given time. However, you will likely not get your industry-specific ratios from there. Instead, you will need to go to old school and simply track them in Excel or Google Sheets. If you want a more advanced option, you could put them into a BI tool like Tableau or Domo.

---

[13] "QuickBooks®: Official Site | Smart Tools. Better Business." *Homepage, Quickbooks*, https://quickbooks.intuit.com/ (accessed on January 1, 2020).

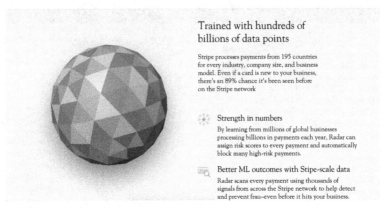

Trained with hundreds of
billions of data points

Stripe processes payments from 195 countries
for every industry, company size, and business
model. Even if a card is new to your business,
there's an 89% chance it's been seen before
on the Stripe network

Strength in numbers
By learning from millions of global businesses
processing billions in payments each year, Radar can
assign risk scores to every payment and automatically
block many high-risk payments.

Better ML outcomes with Stipe-scale data
Radar scans every payment using thousands of
signals from across the Stripe network to help detect
and prevent frau–even before it hits your business.

Figure 3.14 Stripe Radar homepage[14]

What's the Best Way to Detect and Combat Fraud?

Fraud is a major issue for any industry that processes payments on a significant scale. While this is a never-ending battle, advancements in machine learning are helping companies get ahead.

The best way to get started in this area is to choose the right payments provider. Companies like Stripe have created specific products like Stripe Radar (Figure 3.14), which take advantage of the billions of transactions that flow through their network. If this isn't an option, you can explore options like Riskified and Signifyd, which layer on top of your existing payment infrastructure.

If your company is large enough, you can also explore building your own machine learning fraud detection models. While this may seem like a huge project, the ROI behind these systems is usually quite clear.

How Do We Reduce Errors and Technical Issues in Our Operations?

In this category, we want to reduce the amount of technical errors and overall issues in your operations. Let's use software companies as our example in how to reduce technical issues.

---

[14] "Stripe: Radar | Canada." *Homepage, Stripe*, https://stripe.com/en-ca/radar (accessed on January 1, 2020).

Figure 3.15 JIRA[15]

These companies need basic bug-tracking options like JIRA (Figure 3.15), Gitlab, or AWS X-Ray. You can also look into test automation tools which can automatically surface issues before publishing new versions of your code. Options like Sauce Labs, Browserstack, and LambdaTest fit this category. Any company that has digital properties like websites can also benefit from these tools.

Other IT teams can look into options like DataDog, CircleCI, and Amazon CloudWatch for more flexible ways of monitoring technical performance.

What's the Best Way to Increase Customer Satisfaction?

In this category, we want to improve the customer experience, typically after they have purchased your products or services. The most common tool here is a ticketing system that keeps track of custom questions or complaints. You could also expand that into a full-blown CRM system.

Zendesk (Figure 3.16), Freshdesk, Salesforce Service Cloud, Intercom, and Live Agent are all solid options in this space. You want to look for a tool that can work across multiple channels (e-mail, SMS, mobile) while still making it seamless for customers to get help.

---

[15] "Jira | Issue and Project Tracking Software | Atlassian." *Homepage, Atlassian* https://atlassian.com/software/jira (accessed on January 1, 2020).

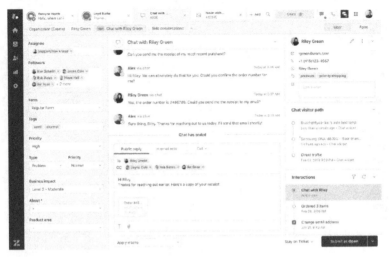

Figure 3.16 Zendesk support[16]

How Do I Keep My Management Team Informed?

Our final category is around keeping management teams informed on what is going on within their company. You need to remember that executives are busy and information needs to be summarized and filtered for them.

I don't recommend a specific tool; instead, work on summarizing the most important KPIs in a dashboard. This could be done using the BI tools mentioned before (Tableau, Domo, PowerBI, etc.) but strive to provide this information in multiple formats. Some executives will want an e-mail summary while others might prefer a physical document. Plan for all these possibilities.

Combining Tools in a Stack

Once you know the two to three questions that you need to answer, you can start to choose tools and combine them into a stack. You're focused on finding a best-in-class tool for solving the category that you care about and which will integrate nicely with your tools.

---

[16] "4 best practices of omnichannel customer support." Blog Post, Zendesk, https://zendesk.com/blog/4-best-practices-omnichannel-customer-support/ (accessed on May 29, 2020).

This integration is becoming increasingly more popular as vendors realize that companies don't want their data to be siloed. Tools that make it easy to take data out through APIs will make these integrations easier. You will also be able to combine tools through the user model we discussed in Chapter 2. Also, see my latest tool recommendations by visiting datamiragebook.com.

Let's now look at how to use guidelines or rules of thumb to sort through hundreds of tools in order to find the two to four options that are worth researching.

Making the Right Choices in a Complex World

There is an unprecedented amount of tools and choosing among them can seem like a full-time job. Even worse, the people leading these projects are typically not fully qualified to make such decisions.

Keep in mind that you don't just need to make one choice. There isn't a single tool that can do it all, so you need to find multiple tools that can play nicely with each other while still being able to generate the insights you care about.

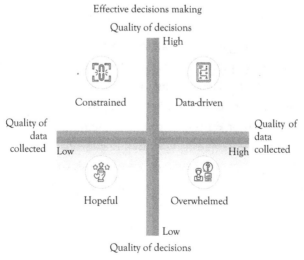

Figure 3.17 Effective decision-making matrix

As you think through your data, don't lose track of the end goal: better decisions. To get here, you need the right data and the right quality of data. We can plot this in a 2 × 2 axis chart (Figure 3.17) to understand how we could optimize for the wrong thing.

In my work, I collaborate with clients to build "stacks." A stack of analytics tools typically includes two to four tools, all of which fulfill a different role. For example, we may have one tool designed to help us understand the performance of marketing campaigns and another tool for understanding how customers use our product.

Building stacks is tricky because you're trying to create an ecosystem that's harmonious. Most companies don't have much experience doing this so they stumble through this process. They end up choosing the wrong tools, wasting engineering resources, and missing out on growth opportunities.

In this chapter, I'll help you create an analytics stack or upgrade your existing one. I'll talk about specific tools but since I can't cover every option under the sun, I'll instead provide you with three guidelines for how to speed through this selection process.

These are the same guidelines that I recommend to my clients when choosing tools. They are meant to help you cut down the research time while still making the right choices for your future.

Guideline #1: Focus on Production-Ready Options

Any given software category might have 20 to 50 options but only a small minority of those are "production-ready." This means that the software vendor has done the hard work of figuring out how their software will scale to the demands of millions of users or data points.

Skip any startups or early-stage companies unless they offer something that is extremely unique or noncritical to your analysis. Your company shouldn't have to worry about software downtime or dealing with slow-loading interfaces. There are bigger challenges where you will need to spend your limited resources and time.

Guideline #2: Look for Industry-Specific Track Records

Software companies will typically focus on specific industries and develop expertise unique to that segment. When choosing tools, look for options that are typically already used by companies within your industry. This isn't the time to reinvent the wheel; instead, you're looking for software vendors that will understand your use cases.

For example, technology companies in the financial industry (known as fin-tech) tend to have strict requirements for where and how they store their data. Software tools that serve this industry will understand this and have developed features solely to solve these concerns.

Guideline #3: How Responsive Are They?

Even the best software tools will fail at times and this is where you will need support from the vendor. Working with a responsive team can make all the difference when it comes to day-to-day problems. This can be tricky to gauge but you can get an initial idea from how the company handles sales demos and questions.

Are they organized in their sales process or does it seem random? If you send them a question, do they respond in a timely manner (24 to 48 hours)? This is something that can still be a problem even if you're on enterprise plans and have a dedicated person assigned to your account.

I have personally worked with customer success teams that take days to answer any question, no matter how simple or complex. This can leave you stranded or stuck in your analysis. This is a deal breaker, especially if you're committing to six-figure contract deals.

Based on these three guidelines, narrow down your list of choices to two to four options in each major category that are relevant to your company. In the next section, I will show you our "Assumption Scoring," a framework for easily comparing multiple options and finding the best option for your company.

Scoring Your Assumptions

Once you narrow your choices down to two to four options, you're ready to use our "Assumption Scoring" framework for making the best choice for your company.

We started doing this with clients a few years ago and it's been quite effective. We will use the template in Figure 3.18 for each category we care about and the two to four options you have.

We'll start by getting pricing estimates for current and future usage. This will depend on each tool but can be by event count, unique users, or team members who use the product. Find something that is consistent across all of your options.

Next, we'll list the features we really care about. For example, we might be interested in how easy it is to create reports, integrations with other tools, and specific industry expertise. I typically recommend 5 to 10 features at most here.

You can then score each feature out of 5 in terms of how important it is to your company. Not all features will have a priority of 5, as that

Features	Importance	Segment/ amplitude X out 5	amplitude/ GTM X out 5	Heap X out 5
Visual tagging - Web	5	5	5	5
Visual tagging - Mobile	5	0	0	5
Auto data collection	5	0	0	5
Nimbleness	5	2	3	5
Corss plarform tracking	3	5	5	5
Core reports	5	5	5	4
Advanced reports	3	5	5	2
Ease of use	4	4	4	3
Warehouse integration	3	5	1	5
Long term fit	2	3	4	4
Score				
Potential score		200	200	200
Total score		126	122	176
Fit score		64%	61%	88%
Assumptions				
Excluded GA/Firebase due to pack of product analytics reports				

Figure 3.18 Assumption Scoring framework example

would defeat the purpose of prioritization. This is where you start making compromises with what is necessary versus what is simply nice to have.

Finally, you will score each tool out of 5 for each feature based on how well you think that tool fulfills that requirement. This number will come out of your research, demos with a sales person, and your overall gut feeling.

At the end of this process, you'll have a quantitative score for each option and one will be higher than the others. Pricing is also part of the overall decision making but not of the scoring.

What clients like about this score is that it makes it easier to see which of the two to three options is a better fit for their company. I say fit because while you'll see that no individual tool will get a 100 percent score, there is always an option that is the best fit for your particular needs.

After this process, you will end up with one option for each category and be ready to start implementing. However, before you start writing any code, let's spend some time talking about foundations and how to build one that can grow and evolve alongside your company.

Building a Strong Foundation and Long-Term Bets

Companies can get lost in the excitement of new tools and possibilities and forget about the future. A strong analytics foundation will save you significant resources down the line but you need to get this right from the beginning.

When I talk about data foundation, I'm talking about two things: who owns your data and how easily you can move it around.

Let's start with data ownership. You want to avoid having your data locked in silos or specific vendors. The ideal solution here is to have a data warehouse (or data lake) into which all of your data flows. This is a database or storage that your company alone controls.

Flowing data into a data warehouse can vary in difficulty. If you implement a tool like Segment.com or mParticle, you will easily be able to flow your data anywhere. Otherwise, you might need to write custom integrations (typically ETLs) to get this job done.

Some vendors also make this easier than others, though most are now moving in the direction of data freedom through APIs. Realistically speaking, it might take your team months or years to get all of your data into one place.

The second problem is data portability. You may have your data in one place but if you can't easily move it around, it's almost worthless.

You can improve your data portability in a few ways. The user model that we talked about in Chapter 2 is a key factor. If you work on unifying all user data around persistent user IDs, you will always have a consistent data model.

Tools will care about different user IDs but if you follow my recommendations, you will have multiple options that can work such as database IDs, e-mails, and anonymous IDs.

The second thing that can help your data portability is having an easy way to query and export data. Team members who know SQL can work with almost anything but you need to think about nontechnical folks. They need an interface that makes it easy to build a query and export data into a portable format like CSV or Excel.

Tackling these two challenges will require an upfront investment but you will thank yourself down the line. Think about the next 10 tools you will need to implement and not just the one you need to get done in the next few weeks.

Who Is Protecting Your Data?

Data privacy is an important topic that doesn't tend to be popular within companies. The people who advocate this (usually legal departments) are treated as obstacles that are preventing growth.

However, this is quickly changing. It seems like there is a new data breach every week and we are in the beginning stages of regulation. Laws like GDPR in the European Union are the seeds that will eventually govern how companies collect and store data.

This means that spending some time thinking about how to protect your data is a sound investment in avoiding future litigation and loss of customer trust.

The foundation work that I talked about earlier will help you with your data privacy efforts. The biggest issue companies have when it comes to data privacy is that they don't know what data they are collecting, how they store, or who is accessing it.

Instead of imposing draconian limitations, you can focus on centralizing your entire data strategy. Having a single place where all data flows into (e.g., a data warehouse) can give you a clear overview as to what data you currently have.

Once again, tools like Segment.com and mParticle are building tools that make it easy to see this data flow while limiting the flow of sensitive PII to specific tools.

Implementing the right tools for your team will also make it easier to manage your data. For example, it's common for teams to rely on spreadsheets to analyze data. However, where are these spreadsheets being stored? This is something that could be solved by implementing a self-serve tool that can handle most of these use cases and educating your team on proper disposal of temporary data spreadsheets.

Finally, we have regulations like GDPR. Complying will involve multiple teams (including legal) who need to amend privacy policies, technical teams who can confirm what data they collect, and business teams who are typically using the data.

From a technical perspective, investing in the creation of internal APIs for deleting user data makes sense. You can build tools that make it easy for someone to delete or scrub any user deletion requests across your entire data infrastructure.

All of this involves thoughtful planning and actual investment of technical resources. The rewards may not be obvious but the alternative of data breach will be even more costly.

Conclusion

We started this chapter by focusing on questions rather than tools. By figuring out the most important question categories for your team, you can then use my three guidelines and the "Assumptions Scoring" framework to find the best tools for your business.

Beyond specific tools, spend time thinking about your data foundation, which will make it easier to truly own your data and comply with data privacy regulations, whether they're internal policies or external ones like GDPR.

You're now ready to start implementing your data strategy. This is an area that requires a solid understanding of politics and negotiation and a certain amount of empathy. I'll help you to effectively work with your engineering team and make implementations a breeze.

Chapter Summary

- Focus on answering questions for your business and not tools. The former is what you're after.
- No single tool will ever do everything you need, so you need to combine them into a stack. Focus on getting compatibility within your tools.
- When researching tools, use my guidelines to filter your list and then compare them using the Assumption Framework.
- Focus on building a strong foundation from day 1 by owning your data and ensuring that you can easily move it around.
- Privacy matters and you need to consider how your business will protect its data and comply with regulations like GDPR and CCPA.

CHAPTER 4

Driving Successful Implementations, on Budget and on Time

Expect the best, plan for the worst, and prepare to be surprised.
—Denis Waitley

The project was done. My client was informing me over the phone that our project was officially done and we wouldn't continue working together. By any measure, the project had failed. We didn't accomplish any of the objectives that we initially talked about despite doing our best for three months.

Projects can fail for a multitude of reasons but this one failed because we didn't get the buy-in from the engineering team. Unbeknown to me, my client (from the marketing team) didn't have the best relationship with the CTO. I didn't do enough to repair this relationship and it ended up halting our entire project.

These lessons stick with me, even years after they happened. Implementation is when you get to really see how much a company cares about data. This is a critical juncture in our journey and one where companies need a lot of help.

Let's start by looking at the major reasons why implementations tend to fail and how you can start preparing.

Why Implementations Fail

Implementation is where the rubber meets the road in our data plan and we start to actually work on hard things. Formulating the strategy, picking tools, and talking about all the wonderful things that could happen are relatively easier.

The bulk of my early consulting work in my practice was centered around implementations. I got really good at figuring out how to drive projects forward, dealing with common issues, and preventing them from ever arising in the first place.

Based on my experience, I think there are five major categories of problems that you will face during the implementation.

1. Getting everyone onboard
2. Establishing the correct ownership and accountabilities
3. Proper planning of your data schema
4. Designing the appropriate budgets
5. Defining the right metrics for success

Let's look at each area and how you take the right preventive and contingent actions to deal with each one.

Getting Everyone Onboard, Even Engineers

Some of my clients have joked that I function as their "Data Marriage Counselor" which is a role I'll be talking about in later chapters. The joke isn't far from reality. There is a natural friction between different teams at companies as they try to balance their objectives and priorities.

Data is something that benefits all teams and requires a team effort to get it right. This is true even of organizations that have dedicated data teams. You might have a few individuals that drive the strategy forward but you will need the support of every team in the organization at some point.

In particular, you will need to have a good relationship with your engineering or technical team. I constantly find myself in meetings with representatives from marketing, product, and the engineering teams where you could cut the tension with a knife. Before we can ever talk about implementation plans, we need to be sure that we have a working relationship. Whenever I skip this step or assume that things are fine, it always comes back to bite me in the ass later on.

That being said, let's look at how you can get different teams onboard by focusing on their self-interest (what they care about) and how to make their life easier.

Getting Engineering or Technical Teams Onboard

Engineering teams care about the security of the product, the technical stability, and avoiding pointless work, for example, implementing tools that no one ever uses. There's always more work than capacity which means these teams are usually overworked and tight on time.

The goal when working with engineering teams is to make the implementation work as easy as possible. You need to provide a clear technical tracking plan (which we will cover later), a final list of tools, and a clear direction of what you want. Be open to any feedback that they might have but this will be a choice on their part and not a responsibility.

A common situation that arises is when nontechnical teams (marketing, product, etc.) are interested in getting access to better data but they feel uncomfortable making tool selections or anything that resembles a technical choice. They then ask the engineering team to research the available options and make recommendations. This then leads to things falling to the wayside as engineering don't have spare time to research things.

In my client projects, I always invite engineering teams to join our calls and provide their feedback but the bulk of this is optional for them. I also make it clear whether a call or meeting is specifically for them and if we don't have any technical items to discuss, they are free to hop off the call early.

That being said, there are a few things that they will have to figure out for you such as:

- Technical choices on how to best capture data, for example, client side libraries, backend libraries
- How to best store any tracking code
- Limitations on what could be reasonably captured

Finally, there are a few benefits that you can cite when getting this team onboard. If the data is implemented properly, there could be less work for them in the future. They would also be contributing to the overall business by helping marketing and product teams do their jobs more efficiently. The data itself could also include metrics around technical performance, common errors, and bug detection.

Engineering is one of the most important teams that you need to get onboard so make sure that this relationship is solid.

Getting Legal or Compliance Teams Onboard

Legal teams will be involved at any company of a certain size and when working in specific industries like banking. They care about any issues that could arise with the data such as leaks, breaking of privacy laws, and future lawsuits.

Lawyers will admit that the safest route for any company is to simply shut down and don't do anything. That is 100 percent guaranteed to be effective but isn't very practical. On the other hand, you don't want to dismiss legal teams for two reasons. First, their concerns are typically valid and second, they can sway incredible power over what you can and can't do. I have seen entire projects be put on hold because the legal team wasn't able to support it.

When you meet with legal teams, be prepared to answer the three following questions at a minimum:

- How are you protecting your data?
- How are you working on preventing issues?
- How will you ensure that these guidelines stay up to date?

You need to be clear as to what data you're tracking, where you're sending it, and who can access it. It's important to know exactly where data is stored geographically, who controls that server, and what are their security procedures.

Have a plan for preventing issues by limiting certain data such as PII, customer credit cards, and social security numbers from ever leaving your servers. You also need to have the ability to limit who can access certain data, enforce two-factor authentication, and monitor usage.

Finally, schedule events to review all of these guidelines to ensure that they are being followed. Depending on your industry and the strictness of your legal teams, you'll have different levels of security.

Compliance teams want to know that you thought about the worst case scenario, put a plan in place for dealing with it, and are being mindful of any potential issues. You will also have to compromise on what data you want to track so be ready to have some things be vetoed from your plan.

Getting Marketing Teams Onboard

Marketing teams care about the costs of their campaigns, the ability for them to execute quickly, and the freedom to be creative. This is a team that doesn't need much convincing but be aware of what they need to make the most out of data.

Any data for the marketing team will be focused on helping reduce their campaign costs, improving how they report on the data, and lower any amount of manual labor which tends to be a lot for most marketing teams. If you can provide tools that make experimentation, such as A/B testing, easier, that's a big win.

Focus on providing the appropriate training and support. Marketing teams are also quite busy and are unlikely to self-learn a tool on their own. Training, which we will discuss later on, will be critical to help them adopt the data.

Getting Product Teams Onboard

Product teams care about building better products and increasing customer satisfaction and better understanding of their users. Like marketing, this is a team that doesn't need much convincing.

Focus on helping them use data to tie outputs to outcomes, increase user engagement, and reduce the overall amount of "failure" work. Failure work refers to any feature that is released that fails to get traction with the user base.

You will also need to provide a comprehensive training plan to help these teams adopt the data and the tools you end up implementing.

Getting Sales Teams Onboard

Sales teams care about closing deals, talking to prospects, and reducing manual labor. This is one of the teams where data can play a significant role but you will have major roadblocks to overcome.

Any data that is given to sales teams needs to immediately be useful against their quota. This team isn't interested in mining the data for useful insights; they have other things they could be doing. Be conservative in the data that you ask the sales rep to input and work on minimizing this as much as possible.

Getting Management Onboard

Management teams care about the overall health of the company, how teams are performing, and their progress toward the expectations set for investors or shareholders. This team also doesn't need a lot of convincing but work on getting their support in the form of resources and direction.

When it comes to benefits, talk about offering better visibility into what is going within the company, higher accountability within teams, and the freedom to make better decisions. Most executives will simply want summaries that tell what they need to know but you will come across some executives who actually want to play around with the data. Make sure that this is an option and offer training to make it easier.

Getting Everyone Else Onboard

I can't cover every possible team but you can follow these general guidelines for any team that I missed. People care about doing their job better, spending more time on things that matter, and reducing the uncertainty that comes from trying new things.

Data can help people make better decisions on how to spend their time and resources which is a big win for any time. It can also make it easier to measure the impact of their work for themselves and other teams. Finally, knowing that you're on the right track can help reduce overall stress.

Regardless of what team you need to get onboard, focus on what they care about and how they will benefit from the data. This will make their (and your) work life much easier. Learn how to get commitment from other teams (and not just compliance) by visiting datamiragebook.com.

Ownership, Not Delegating

The second category of problems arises from a lack of clear ownership. If someone doesn't own something, it is more likely to fall through the cracks. Let's look at the different owners to consider. The same person could have different roles but it should be clear that they are owning specific areas.

Who Owns the Overall Project?

You need someone to drive this entire project forward. I'm usually that person for my larger clients and this entails following up with people, unblocking people, and keeping the momentum going. You might also have an executive champion who is able to get major teams onboard but isn't necessarily driving the project forward.

Who Owns the Technical Component?

You also need someone to own the technical side of the plan. This is typically someone in the engineering team who can assign resources and prioritize this work within their sprints. Having a good relationship with this person is key.

Who Owns Other Areas?

Ownership doesn't end when the implementation is done. You will need someone to take ownership of the many things that follow including:

- Legal and compliance
- Training specific teams and individuals
- Documenting best practices
- Answering day-to-day questions
- Providing support to teams as they adopt the data
- Adding new tracking to the data
- Fixing issues

Proper Planning of Your Data Schema

A data schema is the underlying structure of your data. The concept is quite simple especially once you see it in detail but designing the correct data schemas can be tricky. I learned how to properly do this after running through the process over 100 times and seeing all the gaps and mistakes that I made along the way.

I have come to understand that data schemas are the secret sauce behind good. Bad data schemas will make your data almost worthless, hard to work with, and even hard to explain. We are talking about this now because we first needed to get the strategy out of the way (the 3Ps) and we needed to choose our tool stack.

Data schemas have three fundamental concepts to understand and master:

1. Events
2. Event properties
3. User attributes

Events are the actions that your users or customers take and that you want to track. This can include signing up for your product, purchasing a t-shirt, or even viewing a page. Event properties describe that action in more detail. It might tell us more information about the t-shirt like its color, price, and style. Finally, user attributes describe the user itself and can include things like their name, e-mail, gender, and how many t-shirts they have bought in total.

At the center of the data schema is the user. We should always think from the perspective of the user and how we can attach things to the user. So we attach events, user attributes, and more to a user who we can identify by their name, e-mail, or something else. We are effectively talking about John Smith and everything John did with our business.

Some companies are used to anonymous data where you're simply looking at data points. This is fine in some scenarios but to really make the most out of your data, you need to be able to look at it by its individual users.

When you design your data schema, you want to interact with your business or product like a regular customer would. This means starting with your website and moving along the customer journey. As you take every step, record that action and any details that could be helpful. For example, my initial recording of actions would look like this for a software product:

- Visited website home page
- Visited website pricing page

- Visited website sign-up page
- Created an account by authenticating through my Google account
- Completed my profile by adding my name, phone number, uploading a profile picture, and selecting my industry
- Invited three of my coworkers to join me in this product

All of these actions will become events, event properties, and more. Let's take the three bullet points for account creation. Our event for this action can look like this:

Event Name: user sign-up
Event Properties:

- Authentication type: Google
- E-mail: ruben@practicoanalytics.com
- Name: Ruben Ugarte

You can see that my event captures the general action, for example, signing up, and then I use event properties to capture more information about this action. Anything that could be useful will become an event property.

At the same time, I can also set some user attributes so I can use them. This would include:

- Authentication type: Google
- E-mail: ruben@practicoanalytics.com
- Name: Ruben Ugarte
- Sign-Up Date: March 27, 2020

You'll notice that some user attributes seem to be duplicates of the event properties. This is by design because some tools require both and some tools are unable to analyze some of these. This duplication won't always be there but it's also not a problem to have it.

As we continue this process, we will end up with a document, typically a spreadsheet, that summarizes our entire data schema. You can quickly end up with hundreds of events so here are some best practices when designing your schema.

Use Global Names as Much as Possible

Since we have the ability to capture event properties, we can rely on more global names whenever possible. This means that instead of sending multiple events like user sign-up via Facebook, user sign-up via Google, and user sign-up via e-mail, we can instead send a global event of "user sign-up" and use an event property to specify if it was Facebook, Google, or e-mail.

Pick a Naming Convention

Your schema should have a consistent naming convention which simply means how you spell out the actual words. An example of a naming convention would be to use underscores and lowercase. Our example event would become "user_sign_up." The whole word is lowercase and we replaced all spaces with underscores.

Keep in mind that "user_sign_up" and "user sign up" are both different to most software tools out there. You might think they are the same but computers don't. Pick a naming convention and stick with it. I'm personally a big fan of camelCase for event names, event property names, and user attributes and then letting the actual values, for example, facebook or google, be lowercase.

Be Consistent in Your Naming

Besides the naming convention, be consistent in how you name things. If you create an event property called "authentication_type" and this comes up in another event, don't create a new one called "type_authentication." Be consistent and use the existing one. Anything to do with money could be captured as "amount" for example. This makes it easier for people to learn the schema because they will know that data they can expect.

Edit, Edit, Edit

The main benefit of doing this is on a spreadsheet is that you can edit ruthlessly; aim to implement less instead of more. Some companies recommend implementing five events or some low number to begin with.

Figure 4.1 Data schema example in Google Sheets

I think an arbitrary number doesn't work in the real world but implement less than you think. Part of editing also means prioritizing what gets implemented first.

Designing the right data schema in the first place will make it easier to stay organized in the future especially as the tracking grows.

In Chapter 3 we spoke briefly about CDPs like Segment.com and mParticle. These tools offer a great solution for data abstraction which is relevant for our data schema (Figure 4.1). Tools will change, which means you want to strive to make your data schema as portable and global as possible. You will need to implement things that are unique for your tools but overall data abstraction is the goal.

The document that you see here is a great way to start your implementation efforts but they aren't the best solution for managing your existing data or helping people see what data is available. For that purpose, I recommend that you stick to your actual tools which tend to have ways to visualize your data schema. I find it's better to be as close as possible to the data source when seeing what data is available.

Designing High-Impact Budgets

Another major issue that companies run is paying too much for tools. It's easy to get swayed into six-figure contracts based on potential and how much a tool will help your company. Reality isn't always so easy which is why I tend to come across companies who are spending significant money for tools they don't even use.

I can't tell you how much to spend because that differs for each company. Instead, I can give you the same principles that I use with my clients.

Choose Tools Based on Facts, Not Emotions

Don't fall in love with tools. Instead, use the Assumption Scoring framework from the previous chapter to weigh the pros and cons and get a better objective as to how well a tool fits into your stack.

Prioritize Costs Based on Importance to Business and Focus

Based on your strategy, prioritize those areas first. This may mean that you spend more money helping you figure out your acquisition costs than you do trying to figure out retention. There's enough time to tackle everything over the long term but you're limited in the short term.

Be Conservative in Long-Term Use and Aggressive in Short-Term Adoption

When choosing tools, assume that you'll have a conservative adoption of its functionality. Don't think that everyone in your team will learn and be up to speed on using it over the next 30 days. This will limit how much you commit or if you sign up for that pricey enterprise deal.

In the short term, be aggressive in getting your team to adopt it. Ensure you have the right training and that people are spending the necessary time to learn a tool. Let the tool be the limit and not your people.

Monthly over Annual Pricing in the Beginning

If you aren't sure how well something will perform, go with the monthly pricing. It's really hard when my clients come to me to help them with tools only to discover they are stuck in annual deals. That forces my hand and it means I'm forced to work with whatever they have instead of finding the best solution for them.

This isn't always possible, especially for larger organizations. If you're negotiating an enterprise deal, do your best to go through trial runs, demos, and test data. Even trying a tool for 30 days with limited data can give you a general sense of how well this will perform within your organization.

Calculate the Value per Insight

While data is seen as "obvious," you can try to put a price to the value of your data strategy. In some situations, I have helped companies try and determine the value of their insights. The formula is simple but you need to make a few assumptions on how to categorize what you're learning from your data (Figure 4.2).

Consider the revenue that an insight generated and could generate. You can then take into account the reduced costs and time saved. Finally, multiply your answer by a qualitative impact which could be things like confidence and reducing uncertainty.

This isn't a magic formula but it forces companies to think about what they are actually learning from your data. Is there any tangible value or are you simply playing with numbers?

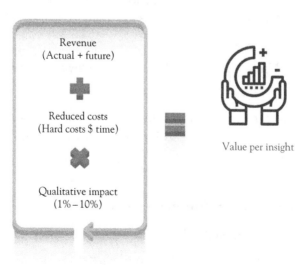

Figure 4.2 Value per insight

The Right Metrics for Measuring Success

Our fifth category is around measuring success. It takes to implement a data strategy and even more time to start seeing the benefits. It is important to use metrics for measuring success along the way. These are some of the questions that I use with my clients.

Is the Implementation Progressing Steadily?

Slow isn't bad but it should be steady. If you can't seem to make progress, you need to explore why this is the case. You might be lacking the right internal support or you might lack the right ownership.

Is the Data Accurate (in Any Amount)?

Having limited but accurate data is better than having a large amount of inaccurate and corrupt data. Accuracy isn't just limited to the technical realm as we will see later on in this book.

Are You Constantly Adding New Tracking Fixes and Additions?

Your first implementation won't be perfect by design. This is an iterative process which means constantly adding new things on a regular basis.

Are People Using the Data in Their Day-to-Day Lives and Meetings?

Once you have data and you have started your training, people should be using it on a day-to-day basis. Look for conversations that mention the data or for presentations that take advantage of the new data.

Are You Progressing in Your Analytics Maturity?

Over the long term, you will progress within your analytics maturity model. In simple terms, you start by focusing on data that tells you what happened, typically referred to as "Descriptive Analytics." You eventually evolve into data that tells you what will happen or "Prescriptive

Analytics." We will cover more about machine learning and data science in future chapters.

Once you implement and start collecting data, it's time to move to some of my favorite work: actually using the data. We'll start by looking at how to create reports and dashboards.

Chapter Summary

- Implementations can fail for a variety of reasons but you can anticipate most of them.
- Getting everyone onboard is one of the most critical steps for any team. Pay special attention to engineering teams.
- Every implementation should have clear owners on the business and technical side. These persons are responsible for driving the project forward.
- Data schemas are the secret sauce to good data and they are designed before any code is ever written.
- Be conservative in long-term use and aggressive in short-term adoption of tools.
- Use the right metrics for measuring the progress of your data implementation.

CHAPTER 5

Creating Reports That People Actually Understand

The greatest value of a picture is when it forces us to notice what we never expected to see.

—John Tukey

One of my favorite childhood movies is *Minority Report*[1] where Tom Cruise plays the role of a police officer who is able to use data to apprehend criminals before they commit their crimes. The movie is visually impressive but the image that sticks with me even to this day is when Tom Cruise is operating the crime prediction machine.

This is how I think some companies believe their reports should be. There's a special room within your office where all the numbers relevant to your company are visible in real time and anyone can come in and access them. We read about "war rooms" earlier but those are the exception and not the norm.

While I admit that this will be incredibly cool and would fulfill a childhood dream, I don't believe this is very practical. Humans have an amazing capacity to consume data but not the kind that we are discussing in this book. For people to actually use data reports, they need to be designed in a certain format while following fundamental principles. This is what we are discussing in this chapter.

What Great Reports Look Like

Building reports is a natural end point for analytics projects but they are actually a critical handoff point for companies. Up to this point, data was either theoretical in the form of a strategy or highly technical in the form

[1] Spielberg, S. June 19, 2002. *Minority Report.* Manhattan, NY: New York City, Film.

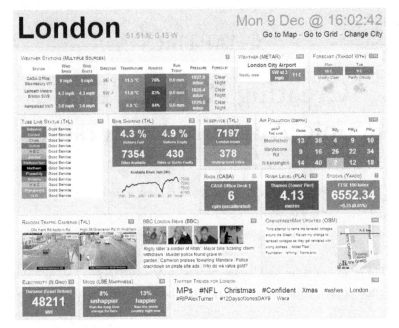

Figure 5.1 **An overcomplicated dashboard[2]**

of implementation plans. This is where data starts to become useful for the majority of people within your organization.

This means that you need to build the right reports that will leave the correct first impression. You don't want your first report to be something like Figure 5.1.

People will feel overwhelmed and less likely to actually see why they should even spend time figuring out this data stuff. Keep in mind that most of the people who will consume these reports are busy and don't have time to "figure things out." You need to make it as easy as possible for someone to open a report, learn something new, and take action on it.

I created a handy concept that I call Small Data for thinking about how much information to include in a report. If you give someone too much data, they will be overwhelmed. If you give someone too little data, they will not feel confident in their decision. The sweet spot (Figure 5.2) is what we are aiming for here.

---

[2] "Dashboard Examples: The Good, The Bad and the Ugly." Blog Post, *Matillion*, https://matillion.com/resources/blog/dashboard-examples-the-good-the-bad-and-the-ugly/ (accessed on January 15, 2015).

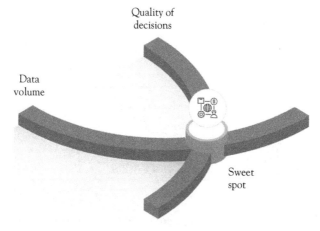

Figure 5.2 Small data

This brings me to another point. Reports will naturally convey information to its reader but I think reports can provide an even more important role: as a feedback mechanism. People and teams are always trying new things within their roles and reports can tell them how they are doing and whether what they are doing is working. This feedback can be extremely valuable if it's provided in the right format.

Before I dive into the principles behind great reports, let me show you some of my favorite examples (Figures 5.3 and 5.4) from my work with clients and that I have come across.

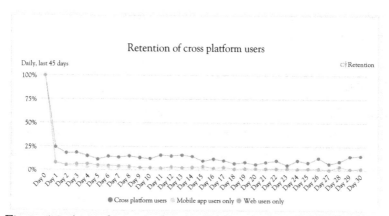

Figure 5.3 A simple report showing the retention rate of different platforms. Colors stand out against each other and we can see at a glance what is going on[3]

---

[3] "Amplitude | Product Analytics for Web and Mobile." *Homepage, Amplitude,* https://amplitude.com/ (accessed on May 7, 2020).

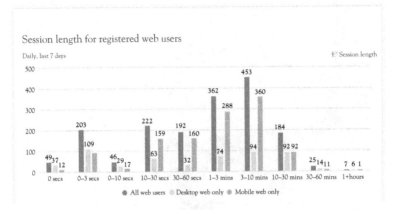

Session length for registered web users

Figure 5.4 Another example of how to show comparisons for different groups of users or customers[4]

You're likely starting to see some of the patterns behind great reports. See more in-depth breakdowns of what great dashboards look like by visiting datamiragebook.com.

Let's now make this clear by diving in the principles behind all of these examples.

Key Principles to Great Reports

The graphs in the following section were all created using a fantastic tool called Datawrapper.[5] I'm using a sample dataset showing the impact of the iPhone (and similar products) of Apple's overall sales.

Visually Appealing

Reports that are visually interesting are more effective because images (in the form of charts) can communicate a story as to what is going on. If you simply show someone a table of raw data, they would need to manually figure out any patterns and interesting data points within this table.

---

4 "Amplitude | Product Analytics for Web and Mobile." *Homepage*, Amplitude, https://amplitude.com/(accessed on May 7, 2020).

5 "Datawrapper." Software App, Datawrapper, https://app.datawrapper.de/ (accessed on January 1, 2020).

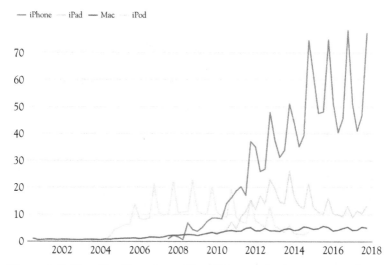

Figure 5.5 Trending line chart. Trend lines make it easy to see how things are changing and could change in the future

A trend line for example can tell us how we are doing in comparison to last year and if we are heading in the right direction (Figure 5.5).

Use the Appropriate Chart

On the topic of trend lines, finding the right chart is critical for conveying the correct story with your data. Here's an overview of common chart types and when you would use them. This isn't a comprehensive list of every possible chart but these are the most common ones that you're bound to run into.

Area Chart

Area charts can be a great way to the growth of an area in relation to something else. Some people might find it easier than visualizing the "empty" space of our trend line example earlier. Be mindful that you need a clear contrast between the categories. You can see in our example in Figure 5.6 that some categories are harder to make out. This could be easier to fix with the right colors but you're likely seeing this graph in black and white which would limit you further.

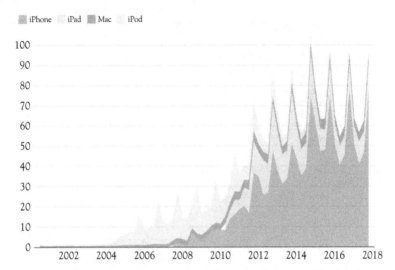

Figure 5.6 Area chart showing the sales growth by specific Apple products

Pie Chart

Pie charts can help you show the split of your data. We can see how big or small each slice is and how they compare to each other. You could also show multiple pie charts next to each other to compare different products and their breakdown. Pie charts are similar to donut charts but they have slight design differences (Figure 5.7).

Bar Chart

Bar charts are another way to compare different categories. Standalone bar charts can be helpful but they become even more useful when you add comparisons. An example would be a comparison of this year's versus last year's performance (Figure 5.8).

Dot Plot

Dot plots can help you see different data points spread out over a range (Figure 5.9). This is helpful if you're interested in seeing individual data points while also seeing them in context to each other. An example of this would be the mortality rate of diseases and how they have changed over time.

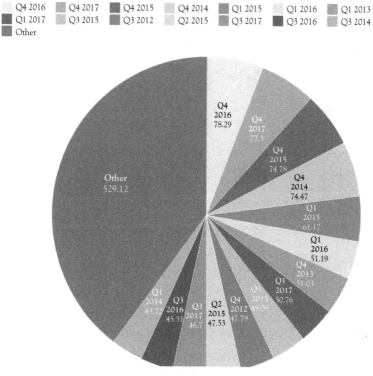

Figure 5.7 Pie chart showing the quarterly breakdown of iPhone sales

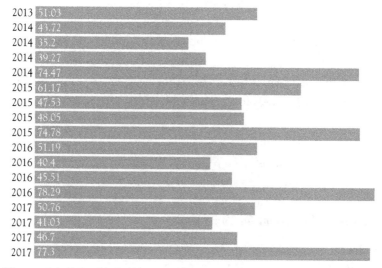

Figure 5.8 Bar chart of just iPhone sales by quarter

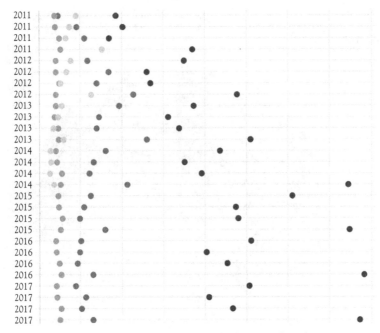

Figure 5.9 Dot plot showing the spread of quarterly sales

Explain Your KPIs

Make sure to explain what your KPIs mean. It's common for me to hear a company talk about "retained users" where everyone uses different definitions. If you're just starting to share data within your company, make sure to clearly explain the formulas behind all reports to avoid any confusion. Over time, these definitions will become common knowledge and you can simplify your reports further by removing them. You can focus on explaining three key ideas in all your reports using DFE:

- Definitions behind all your KPIs
- Formulas for coming up with these numbers
- Exceptions that aren't included in this report

Find the Right Format for Your Audience

Besides the nuts and bolts of what goes inside your reports, it is important to find the right format for your audience. Executives will typically want summaries of the data and might prefer to get those directly to their

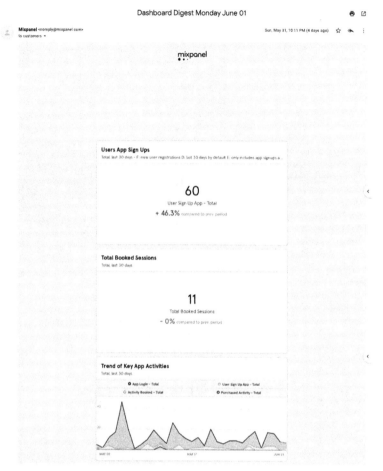

Figure 5.10 E-mail digest can be a great way to get data into a place that everyone checks on a regular basis[6]

e-mail (Figure 5.10). Managers might want the ability to dive into the data and could prefer a link that they could click through in their computers. Talk with your team as to how they would like to see the data and tweak your reports to fit them, not the other way around.

Compare Time Periods

All of your reports should also have built-in comparisons between time periods (Figure 5.11). Numbers without context can be confusing and

[6] "Product and User Behavioral Analytics for Mobile, Web, & More | Mixpanel." *Homepage, Mixpanel*, https://mixpanel.com/ (accessed on February 13, 2020).

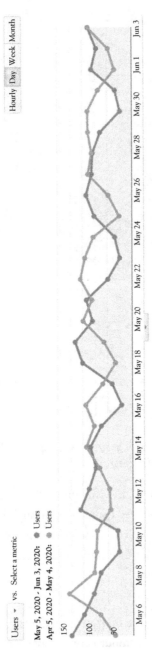

Figure 5.11 Data comparison can provide context to any report[7]

[7] "Analytics Tools & Solutions for Your Business - Google Analytics." *Homepage, Google Analytics,* https://marketingplatform. google.com/about/analytics/ (accessed on February 1, 2020).

downright harmful. Seeing that your team had 50,000 sales last month might be bad but seeing that this was an increase of 25 percent from 40,000 from the previous month starts to add the much needed context. You can compare to the previous time period, for example, last month or last week, or you could compare to the previous year or to a running average, for example, monthly average for the last six months.

Show Change and Segments

Besides the comparison of time periods, also show how a number is changing. The previous example of 50,000 sales could be improved by comparing time periods but it can be further improved by showing a trend line of how sales are trending over the last three months. This could be further improved by showing the most relevant segments that make up this number of 50,000 sales such as countries, products, or marketing campaigns.

Less Is More

Remember that less is more. It's better to start with a shorter report that you can add to over time than to simplify a complex report. Providing people with a handful of key insights is more practical than drowning them with everything they should know.

Designing for Humans, Not Computers

Designing great reports means thinking of the humans that will read them. Computers can process large amounts of data without missing a beat but humans can get easily overwhelmed especially because we are trying to balance our complex lives with this KPI report that you created. Empathy and compassion are helpful when thinking of how people will be consuming your reports.

That being said, here are a few psychological tricks that you can use to make your reports more effective. Keep in mind that your job isn't to tell people what they already know; instead it is to show them something that they might be missing.

Balance Recent Data with Historical Records

We tend to value recent data as more valuable, commonly known as the recency bias. This might mean that we might think an increase in a recent KPI is incredible but it might still be lower than where things were six months ago. Being able to show how current data compares to historical averages is helpful for putting numbers into context.

Focus on ROI, Not Loss Aversion

We also tend to prefer to avoid losing than winning which is known as the loss aversion bias. I have seen many companies skip investing into key campaigns because they couldn't see the clear ROI and instead only saw the downsides. In your reports, it's important to show what kind of realistic ROI is possible and what that means in raw dollars or outcomes.

Be Careful How You Frame Data

How you frame data will determine what kind of conclusion your consumers reach. You could frame a 25 percent increase in sales during your slow season as disappointing because your team achieved 40 percent during the busy season. Any number can be framed to be positive or negative so you need to make some decisions as to what the objective truth is.

Averages Lie, Segments Don't

Averages are popular because they can quickly summarize complex numbers. What is the average revenue per user? What is the average cost to acquire a customer? However, always remember that averages are lying to you and withholding information.

Let's take a recent event, the COVID-19 pandemic, as an example. At the time of this writing, there were 2.2 million reported cases in the world affecting 210 countries. If we calculate the average cases per country, we would get 10,476. The number is technically correct but only 23 countries (or 11 percent) actually have more than 10,000. The average is hiding significant outliers like the United States which has 31 percent of all the reported cases.

Instead, we want to look at segments within our data. This could be things like:

- Geographic, for example, city, region, country
- Demographic, for example, gender, age
- Behavioral, for example, products bought, when they became a customer
- Engagement, for example, customer satisfaction

What's the Story You're Telling

There's a tendency to look at numbers as just objective facts or the truth. In reality, all numbers are constructing a story in the mind of your data consumers. You need to be aware of this story and ensure that this is what you want to be telling. Humans naturally look for stories so a KPI like 50,000 sales isn't just a number. There's a story as to why that number is high or low and how that number is changing.

Break the Confirmation Bias

Reports are also a great opportunity to break the confirmation bias. This is where we actively look for information that confirms our opinion and dismiss any information that contradicts it. If you have team members who seem to think that things are going better or worse than they are, reports can do that. You'll also need to ensure that they also trust the data (a subject for a future chapter).

Separate Correlation and Causation

You can also use reports to answer the question of correlation and causation. This simply states whether something is the cause of something else or merely related. For example, if ice cream sales increase during the summer, is summer the cause of this increase or simply related?

This question is quite tricky to answer but reports allow you to clarify any relationships between your KPIs. We'll discuss this more in a future chapter as we dive into data analysis.

The Difference Between Reports and Analysis

One final point that I would like to make is around the difference between reports and analysis. Reports are meant to give you a summary of what is going on and serve as the beginning of the data analysis process. Data analysis occurs when you convert these raw materials from your reports into insights.

Some reports are designed to get everyone on the same page. An example would be a report for management teams that summarize the performance of the previous month. There's unlikely any data analysis to be taken place here but this report still serves an important role.

An executive might be interested in learning why something happened which would then take us into the data analysis world. We would then need to create new reports where we are able to dig into the data to find the answer to our question.

At the end of the day, reports are tools that people can use to make better decisions but there's always an element of human interpretation that is needed.

Now that we know how to build great reports, it's time to look at how to train your company to use data. This is where we start handing off actual data and the ability for people to query their own data if you build the right data stack.

Chapter Summary

- Reports function as a feedback mechanism showing them the outcome of their decisions.
- Focus on making reports visually appealing, using the appropriate chart, and effective.
- Find the right format for your reports which could be e-mail, a dashboard, downloads, and so on.
- Remember that you're designing for humans, and not computers.
- Reports summarize data for you while data analysis dives deeper into the data to find insights.

CHAPTER 6

The Last Mile: Training

We don't rise to the level of our expectations, we fall to the level of our training.

—Archilochus

There's 26 seconds left on the clock and Russell Wilson is setting up what is likely his last play of the game.[1] The Seattle Seahawks are down by four points and they have a chance to win Super Bowl XLIX. To any observer, it seemed obvious that they would run the ball to Marshawl Lynch, one of the greatest running backs in the game at the time. Instead, Wilson threw a pass that was intercepted, thus ending the Seahawks' chance of winning.

The "last play" would become infamous in the NFL world. Most people thought it was a terrible play. It seems to go against everything that the team had done in the season and even in the game itself. This fumble in strategy ended up being costly for Seattle.

Back in our data world, I see the same issue happen with companies all the time. They are about to win the game after working hard through all the issues in the previous chapters but they fumble their data in the last few yards.

In this chapter, we will start looking at how to work with your team to use data by setting the right foundation through training.

You're Almost There, Don't Fumble Your Data

If you have followed the process up to now, then you're in a great position to tackle training. This is what closes the gap that companies face when

---

[1] "Super Bowl XLIX." Wiki, Wikipedia, https://en.wikipedia.org/wiki/Super_Bowl_XLIX (accessed on June 6, 2020).

they first start becoming more data driven. They will have a few people (sometimes just one or two) that understand the data front and back. They could tell you every little thing that it's being tracked, where it is coming from, and what kind of insights you could get from it.

The rest of the company has no idea what is going with the data and, in some cases, can even feel overwhelmed at all the new tools and reports. The data experts assume that people will just "learn it over time." They will somehow pick up everything they need to know through osmosis and just being around the data.

This is a mistake and the fundamental premise of this book. The technique is straightforward and we can use the process that we have described until it's time to deal with common technical challenges. The actual usage of data is complex because we are dealing primarily with people issues—people's lack of trust, people's lack of technical knowledge, and people's lack of time to learn new things.

If you "fumble the data" like the Seahawks did, you'll end up in an unusual place. Your company will have a high capacity for collecting data but a low ability to actually use it. When I come across companies that are in this position, I instantly know that they have talented technical folks who are passionate about data but are unable to get the rest of their company to match their enthusiasm or knowledge.

That being said, we are going to take everything we know so far around strategy, tools, and our data schema and convert it into a format that makes sense for the rest of the team. This is the time to transfer this knowledge in a way that is actionable and relevant for the rest of the company.

The MTS (Measure Team Skills) assessment from earlier chapters will help you determine how technical you should go in your training and what things you could realistically skip. In this chapter, we will talk about training design and best practices around how to best deliver technical content.

In the next chapters, we will dive deeper into other issues that prevent people from using the data. Training is important because it sets the foundation for everything we will do. We can't solve the other issues if your team hasn't gone through basic training.

Realistic Training Design for Your Team

When I think about training my clients, I typically focus on four areas which will tackle different outcomes. These are four training "tools" that you can deploy:

Group Training: We start with group sessions to go over basic concepts and ideas. These sessions are practical in nature and customized for each team (marketing, product, etc.).

Individual Training: We then move on to individual sessions where we can really dive into specific problems and challenges.

Reactive Training: In this format, I'm reacting to problems that come up as people start using the data and mining for insights.

Documentation: The last step is to create documentation on best practices. This helps capture answers to common questions.

To see a comprehensive training plan involving all four elements, please visit datamiragebook.com.

These four training types would be put into a logical life cycle typically covering three to six months.

When you design the training, you could focus on individual teams and needs (Figure 6.1). For example, I might break up the group training

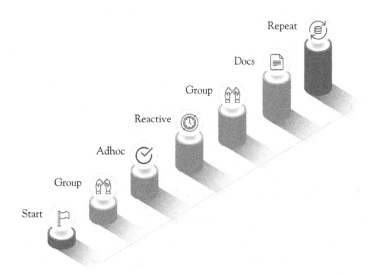

Figure 6.1 Training lifecycle that repeats over time

sessions by team, for example, marketing, product, and sales and then go through individual training sessions with key people from these teams. The more relevant the training, the better.

Try to show instead of telling. For example, if you're explaining how a report works, it is much better to show the report in action with real data and customers from your business than talking about hypothetical situations. This does mean that you might delay certain training until you have enough data.

Assume that people will only pick up a handful of things from any given training session. You can't expect someone to take a one-hour training on a new tool and know everything it does. Design your training around helping people master these handful of ideas.

Finally, training can become an exercise in futility. Spending days and weeks in training is a waste of time in my opinion. I think it's better to teach someone a handful of things, let them out in the wild to use them, and support them along the way. This means I might schedule my group sessions, have a 30-day break where I'm checking in on people one-on-one, and then come back to do another group session to dive into more advanced topics. Shorter and sweet is the goal here.

What Training Success Looks Like Here

As you start going through training, you might wonder if it's actually working. I have seen people that have unrealistic expectations of what their team might do which leads to all kinds of frustration and conflicts. To help you avoid that, let me share three qualitative metrics that you can use to track the impact of your data and how well the data is being adopted.

People Are Building Reports That Answer Their Questions

The first metric revolves around people building or requesting their own reports. This is especially true for companies that set up self-service tools designed for nontechnical folks. The reports and dashboards don't have to be complex but expect a willingness to try and use the data.

Data Is Being Used in Meetings and Presentations

The second metric is whether people are using the data in their meetings and presentations. Again, the complexity of their data usage will vary but seeing slides and comments on "what the data says" is a positive sign of data adoption.

There Is Demand for More Data and Fixing Gaps

The third metric will be an increasing demand for more data and fixes. This one is tricky because I have seen teams that use technical issues as an excuse for not using the data. The data is never accurate or reliable enough so it's not their problem that they can't use it. I will talk about the lack of trust of data in future but seeing a demand for more data is typically a good sign.

Once you're done through training, your work isn't done. In the next chapter, we will take a closer look at the issues that teams run in when they start using data. We'll demystify what data adoption really means and to become truly data driven.

The Difference Between Knowledge and Wisdom

One of the most interesting ideas that I share with clients revolves around knowledge and wisdom. Knowledge is when you know what happened while wisdom tells you what you should do.

You naturally have to work on getting knowledge first but it can be easy to fall into the trap of always wanting to know more. This trap can prevent you from finding wisdom about your company and products.

As you build reports and dashboards, keep this in the back of your mind. Think about how much of what you're learning is knowledge versus wisdom. There's no magic split but if you find that you aren't acquiring enough wisdom, then you need to relook at your overall strategy. You might be caught up in "perfection"—the perfect tool, report, dashboard, and so on.

Chapter Summary

- Training closes the gap between strategy and actual usage. This is how you get people to become more data driven.
- Remember that the technical is straightforward but the people component is complex and messy.
- Design your training around four building blocks: group, individual, reactive, and documentation.
- Focus on teaching people what they need to know to get started and then let them loose in the world. Short and sweet is the goal here.
- Keep in mind the difference between knowledge and wisdom.

CHAPTER 7

Your Biggest Challenge: Actually Using the Data

Better to light one candle than to curse the darkness.

—John Crowley (*Four Freedoms*)

In the last few years, we have seen the rise of "fake news" or at least the perception of them. Of course, this has existed throughout years. Misinformation (by accident or deliberately) isn't something new to the 21st century. I'm also not going to make a political statement about the causes of fake news or who's to blame. I'm more interested in what this says about how we consume data.

There's a general feeling that people just need to "hear the facts." If you can show someone the "truth," they will come around to your cause. We have seen that this is not the case. We all interpret data according to our biases and morph into something that makes sense to us. This is relevant because the same thing happens within organizations.

If you did everything right up to this point, you might still run into issues getting data adopted within your company. This simply means that people are using it. In this chapter, we'll explore the different reasons why individuals and teams reject data and how to work with them. These are valid issues that need to be addressed and a critical part of your data journey.

Demystifying Data Adoption

Data adoption sounds like a fancy phrase but it is simply the way people actually use data. You would think that using data is the easiest part of any data strategy but I believe this to be the opposite. Figuring out the strategy, choosing tools, implementing, and creating reports are relatively easy compared to actually using the data.

This is because humans are complex and organizations have natural friction points that make it harder for data to be accepted. This is why survey after survey always says the same thing: everyone wants more data, organizations are willing to invest in it but no one has the insights that they need. In fact, for the money and time that is being invested, it doesn't seem that much value is coming out.

This disconnect is what we are going to talk about in this chapter. Everything we have done up to this point can be wasted if we don't actually figure out how to get people to use the data in their daily work lives.

Let's start by talking about what it really means for data to be adopted and used by regular people. You need to understand that this will look different from everyone depending on their technical ability and overall interest in the data. You can't expect that a marketing executive will use data in the same way a marketing manager would.

You'll know that data is being used if you see people creating their own reports (or tweaking existing ones), using data in their regular meetings or presentations, and if you hear people talking about what they learned from the data, what people call "insights."

That's it. This is what you can aim for as a general goal for most of the organization. From there, you'll start to see projects and initiatives that are based on data and you'll come across more decisions that are supported by data.

The exceptions to this goal would be data-only teams whose main work is diving deeper into the data. These teams will need to build advanced reports, build models, and take advantage of machine learning and AI trends.

Once you know these goals, it is important to communicate them internally and let people know when they are hitting them. Coming back to my example of executives versus managers, you will need to manage expectations of how data should be used.

An executive is already quite busy and shouldn't be expected to be diving through the data to find insights. Instead, they should be presented with summaries of the most important insights in a format that makes sense to them. They could also be given the option to play with the data on their own which is something that few executives actually do.

A manager on the other hand should be expected to spend more time digging through the data to find insights. They may need support from a data analyst or a technical person but this is something that should be covered in your data strategy.

Manage expectations on the overall accuracy of the data. Some data is meant to be the "source of truth" and have 100 percent accuracy. This data typically comes from your product databases, payment processors, CRM, or another reliable source.

Other data is meant to be "directionally correct" and may only include 90 to 95 percent of all the data. This data is what you typically see in web analytics, marketing campaigns, and user behavior and is affected by issues like ad blockers, and other technical issues. I have seen companies go down rabbit holes trying to capture the other 5 to 10 percent of data and waste too much time trying to do so. You can still get insights and make decisions with directionally accurate data but there're limits.

Prepare your team for some kind of learning curve when it comes to the data and tools you selected. This will vary depending on the makeup of your team but don't expect everyone in your team to have mastery of the data within weeks. It takes time to get enough "cycles" on the data and see the impact of ideas and changes.

Manage how much time people are spending with the data. It is possible to go into analysis paralysis from too much data or what seems like not "enough" data and avoid making decisions. Strive for making decisions that are "good enough" and perhaps even on the side of aggressive.

Finally, the training on the data shouldn't stop. It will change, however, from high-level ideas into more practical and day-to-day issues. Focus more on the ad hoc, reactive, and documentation training options over time.

This is what data adoption will look like at your company. Let's now look at some of the common scenarios that you will come across. Let's start by talking about "funky data" and how it plagues companies.

Dealing with Funky Data

I'm always surprised at how many companies don't trust their data. They will look at a chart or report and get this uneasy feeling that something is off.

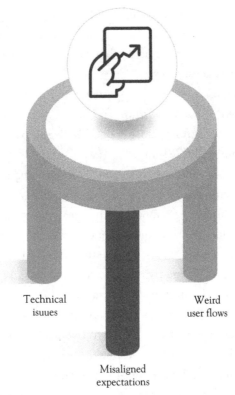

Technical issues — Weird user flows — Misaligned expectations

Figure 7.1 Funky data

This is what I call "funky data." Even though the numbers "seem" right, there is something funky going on (Figure 7.1).

There are multiple reasons why you get funky data but the outcome is the same: if your team can't trust the data, they won't use it. You need to stay on top of issues like this before it spirals out of control. Bringing trust in your data (even across basic numbers) should be one of the top priorities behind any data strategy.

Let me go over three common scenarios that result in funky data and how to solve them.

Scenario #1: Technical Mistakes

This is what most people assume when they come across funky data. Something is wrong with the tool or the data that was collected. The blame is on the technical portion of the data and sometimes even on the engineers who implemented the tracking.

Resolving this scenario will involve checking all numbers against a secondary data source which is trustworthy. For example, if you're looking at the number of first-time purchases in marketing tools, you could compare those numbers against your payment processor which will likely be 100 percent accurate.

You also want to ensure that you're able to compare apples to apples. This means ensuring your reporting uses the same time zone (a common mistake), and the underlying query is the same.

For example, don't assume that all reports use the same definition of a "first-time purchase." One tool might mean the first purchase that the user has ever done while another tool might mean the first purchase done in a 12-month period.

Scenario #2: Misaligned Expectations

The second scenario that leads to funky data is misaligned expectations. This is common in teams that have never had much data, to begin with. They have been operating under assumptions of what their numbers are so when they receive the actual data, they might be disappointed with the results.

If your team assumes that you're getting a 10 percent conversion rate (based on napkin math) and you then get a report that says the conversion rate is 6 percent, you will immediately face resistance to this number.

In this scenario, you will need to spend extra time explaining how the 6 percent was calculated (and triple checked) and why this is the actual number. Over the long term, trends in the data should help realign everyone's expectations.

Scenario #3: Unexpected Calculations

The third scenario revolves around unexpected user flows. Let's go back to first-time purchases and assume that we want to see users who created an account and then purchased a subscription. You then realize that your reports seem to be missing a large chunk of the purchases. What's the deal?

In this case, you might have users who created an account 12 months ago (before the tracking was implemented) but are purchasing the subscription now. These users wouldn't be counted in that specific report.

This scenario involves tracking down these discrepancies and explaining why they happened. Just like scenario #2, you will need to consistently work to explain how the data works and expected limitations. For more resources on Funky Data, please visit datamiragebook.com.

It isn't just funky data that throws people off. You'll need to work against serious psychological biases that affect all of us. We talked briefly about some of these back in the chapter about creating reports but here are a few others.

Anchoring Bias

As people start working with the data, most will have anchors to what numbers should be. Data may prove or disprove this which can lead to people rejecting these numbers. This is one of the cases of funky data.

Clustering Illusion

It is also common for people to see patterns in small amounts of data. They see a handful of users and conclude that certain attributes are more likely to convert or become customers. Your training should provide guidelines for how to think about statistically correct conclusions.

Congruence Bias

This bias can happen when people start thinking about experiments. There can be a tendency to want to prove an idea by testing it directly and avoid thinking of alternatives that could also work. They can also look toward the data to find something that confirms this approach.

Confirmation Bias

Common bias where people are looking for data that confirms their pre-existing beliefs and will dismiss anything that contradicts them.

Overconfidence Effect

Data can also lead to an overconfident bias in certain numbers and outcomes. This is also part of establishing the proper way of analyzing data and coming to conclusions that have sound statistics in place.

All of these can be solved but you will need patience and empathy. I especially see conflicts with technical folks (data analysts, engineers, etc.) who have to help nontechnical folks. This is normal but your organization will need to work through these challenges. Democratizing data isn't hard because of the constraints of technology but because people need support and that support may not always be readily available.

That being said, I also think that companies can benefit from establishing one role that I have served for companies: Data Marriage Counselor. This role specializes in bridging the gap I mentioned above but it can be tricky to set up.

If in Doubt, Establish a Data Marriage Counselor

Some companies will need a lot of internal support when they first start working with data. Trying to offer this support in part-time fashion may not be enough. When my clients hire me, they assume that I will be the liaison between their business teams (marketing, product, sales, etc.) and their technical teams (engineering and data). I'm expected to translate what each team needs and wants and make everyone happy.

I have come to see this role like a Marriage Counselor. I'm not here to pick sides but to simply improve the communication between two people (or multiple teams) and drive toward a positive resolution.

This role can be incredibly valuable for companies who would like to make data a top priority. There are a lot of issues that are made worse by a lack of clear language. Engineers will provide clear instructions on how the data works (from their perspective) but these instructions may not be enough or they may be inappropriate for someone who isn't as technical as they are.

Whoever takes on this role should see themselves as a wise Yoda from Star Wars. You're trying to help people learn how to fish (or use the force if they stay with the same analogy) and this means teaching them practical skills and working with them at their level. However, there will be instances where you will need to fish for them because there are time constraints or other limitations.

Whether you hire for this role or appoint an existing person in your company, look for the following attributes:

- **Business Strategy:** They should understand the overall company strategy and how any given project or request for data is aligned. This is what we might call business acumen or being able to see how all the pieces line up.
- **Technical Skills:** Data is inherently technical but it doesn't mean that this person needs to be a full-blown engineer. They will need to understand all the technical issues that could arise and how they could be solved even if that will be done by someone else.
- **Systematic Problem Solving:** Putting out fires is great but this person should be working to fix the overall system. If data isn't easy to access, they can solve it by providing short-term reports but the long-term solution is to provide easier access for everybody. This is systematic problem solving and not just focusing on solving the immediate requests.
- **People Skills:** Most of the issues with data are people related so this person will need a high level of empathy. Someone is able to easily explain technical concepts in layman terms if particularly helpful.
- **Statistics Skills:** Having a basic understanding of statistics is key especially when helping people come up with conclusions from their data. Statistics can be a technical subject so this would be tied to their overall technical skills.

This is a special role that I think more companies will come to appreciate over time. In some cases, you will also need to hire other roles to support you overall.

Building Trust, One Report at a Time

Your first few months of any data strategy might feel like a war. There are requests coming from everywhere, people are frustrated (and excited), and there doesn't seem to be enough time to get everything done.

In times like this, focus on building trust one report at a time. One dashboard that everyone agrees is valuable or one report for one team. It may not seem like much but doing this consistently will add quite a few reports and dashboard over time.

Focus and celebrate the small wins. Maybe it takes a marketing team less time to measure their campaigns or product teams are able to see how their features are getting adopted. These small wins are crucial for building momentum (psychological and literal) within a company. It gives companies the motivation to work on bigger problems and to allocate the relevant resources.

This is also where your "Process" section from your data strategy will get tested. It's normal to have gaps from your initial design but work to close those gaps quickly. How people consume and use data is a tricky problem but it can be solved with the right process and training.

Let's now move on to best practices when it comes to analyzing data. I'll cover specific workflows that you can use to find actionable insights hidden within your data.

Chapter Summary

- Data adoption simply means how people are using the data to make better decisions.
- Figure out the right expectations for how your team should be using data based on your unique makeup and skills.
- Funky data can happen for multiple reasons but you need to tackle it before it gets out of control.
- Be aware of psychological biases that affect how we all consume data.
- You may also need to appoint a data marriage counselor to help your team make sense of your data.
- Focus on building trust in your data, one report at a time.

CHAPTER 8

Analyzing Your Data and Workflows

Of course. Treasure hunts make much better stories when there's treasure at the end.

—Eric Berlin, *The Puzzling World of Winston Breen*

Despite its obvious value, data analysis isn't where companies spend most of their time when it comes to data. So much time is spent simply trying to organize data (what is sometimes called "data preparation") that it makes it hard for analysis to be the star.

In this chapter, we'll dive deeper into the process of data analysis and how you can apply it to common workflows. Keep in mind that data analysis isn't for everyone. Some people in your organization will simply want summaries (e.g., reports or dashboards). You'll need to understand what each person wants and is able to do when it comes to data.

Let's start by going behind the scenes of data analysis.

Behind the Scenes of How Data Is Analyzed

Data analysis might seem like a mysterious process to outsiders, shrouded in mystery, where you only see the output: insights. In reality, there's a process that all data analysis follows and that any person can learn. Once you understand this process, you can apply it to all kinds of data.

The main thing to realize, however, is that data analysis takes time. It's an exploratory process which means you're digging around the data for insights. You may have a hunch of where the answer is but you might need to structure and organize the data in different ways until you find what you're looking for.

Some people might say that this process is tedious and they would also be correct. The process itself can also feel quite technical which may alienate some people. Regardless of how you currently view data analysis, my job here is to show you a process that makes sense and that you could use if you wanted to. I think every person can benefit from knowing the basis of how to process data as this will apply to any decision that you'll ever make.

Before we ever start any data analysis, there are a few prerequisites that we need to know and understand. First, we should have a solid understanding of the business and product. This means knowing how the business operates, the most important KPIs, and the gears inside a business. Second, we need to understand the customers and how they use and think about the products. Third, we need to understand humans in general to put our data into context.

This last point is something that has come up throughout this book whenever we talk about data. When we look at charts, it can be easy to forget about the humans behind the data points. However, remembering that there are humans behind our data will make it easier to understand it.

If we can see that usage for our product increases in the morning on weekdays and we know that our customers are restaurant managers, we could assume that these people are using our product as part of a daily routine during the beginning of the day. We could confirm this with surveys and interviews.

Once we have our three prerequisites, we can begin the data analysis process which looks like this:

1. **Determine what questions you would like to answer**

   The process will always start by determining what questions we would like to answer. Example questions include "what is the performance of our product over the last few months?" and "what marketing campaigns are bringing the best users?" Good questions make the process easier while bad questions simply take you down rabbit holes. A bad question in this context is one that isn't really relevant to the business or what you're working on.

2. Gather all relevant data

The next step is to gather all relevant data. This may mean downloading the data into forms like Excel and CSV or simply running reports on your analytics tool. It could also mean that you need help from a data analyst or engineer to get this data.

3. Visualize the data to get basic answers

Now that we know what questions we would like to answer and what gathered our data, then we need to start visualizing the data. Don't assume that visualizing means creating complex dashboards. We simply need to organize the data in a way that is readable which could be as simple as a table or a trend line chart. At this step, we simply want to start getting basic answers that we could dig into.

For example, if we are answering the question on the best marketing campaigns, we would want to start by showing all the different marketing campaigns that brought users over the last 90 days (or another date period). This would give us a high-level overview of what happened in relation to our question.

4. Rearrange the data to confirm or reject assumptions

Once we have some basic answers, we'll also have some ideas on where we should dig further. This is where we will start to rearrange the data to confirm or reject assumptions that we have. For example, let's say that we saw that Facebook Ads drove 40 percent of all new users in the last 90 days.

We would now want to dig in further to confirm how much this costs us (cost per new user), which individual ads drove the most users (if any), and how much revenue (or another conversion) was generated from these users. We may discover the Facebook Ads drove the most users but also the least profitable. We may also discover an individual ad was responsible for the bulk of these users in general.

This is where data analysis can get tedious. You may need to keep digging in different ways only to discover nothing useful.

You may also realize that you're missing data and you need to go back and get it.

5. **Come up with conclusions or insights**

Finally, we can come up with conclusions or insights. These insights might need to be further tested before being fully validated. This is especially important for insights where we think that we see causation but there's only correlation. We'll be talking about this in the next chapter but just know that this is normal.

This concludes the data analysis portion but it also starts another process: experiment design. If our conclusion is that Facebook Ads drove the most profitable users, then we should find ways to scale these campaigns. We'll need to run some experiments to see if this conclusion holds true as we ramp up spending. Our next chapter will look at how we can take conclusions (or insights) and convert them into experiments.

This also brings up another point that I see companies struggle with. In a lot of cases, you'll end up with clues and not answers. Executives can easily get tired of hearing "it depends" but in reality, this is what you'll be stuck with. The solution isn't to get better at data analysis but to get faster at testing these conclusions through experiments.

In the next section, I'll show you best practices for how to analyze common areas within a business. I call them "workflows" as a way to encompass everything that might take place when analyzing marketing campaigns or a sales process.

Common Workflows That You Can Explore

After working with over 100+ companies, I have come to see common areas that overlap across companies. In this section, we will take a look at common analysis workflows that you could start applying to your data today. Not every workflow will be relevant to you as my work typically spans multiple industries but you're bound to find a handful of workflows that can help you.

Customer Acquisition

Following our analysis process, there are a few of the questions that can be answered with this workflow:

- What is our overall performance in customer acquisition?
- What are the economics of our customer acquisition?
- What opportunities exist to decrease costs and scale the acquisition of customers?
- The data that will be needed here is as follows:
  - List of all customers or users
  - Demographic information about the users (name, e-mail, gender, location, etc.)
  - Behavioral information about the users (lifetime revenue, what products they use or purchased)
  - Attribution of the source of users in terms of marketing campaign or channel
  - Cost of marketing campaigns and channels
  - 90 days of historical data

Now that we have our questions and initial data, let's get some basic answers. The goal would be to get all of this data into a single table where each record is the individual customer and the columns correspond to the rest of the data. You may need to average out costs of all the users who were attributed to specific marketing campaigns (Figure 8.1).

For this analysis, we'll focus primarily on using pivot tables to summarize our master table. We can run several queries to get the following basic answers:

- Average cost to acquire a customer (CAC)
- Average cost to average lifetime value
- Best performing campaigns in terms of cost or revenue

This will start to give us insights as to what campaigns we should focus on, which campaigns we should stop running, and the overall performance

	A	B	C	D	E	F	G	H
1	User ID	Name	Email	City	Country	LTV	Last Purchase Date	Total Purchases
2	34050	Salley Wages	arreau@att.net	Dallas	United States	$45.00	2/21/2020	3
3	34051	Lovie Ledoux	sonnen@outlook.com	Beijing	China	$32.00	1/23/2020	4
4	34052	Janina Wasden	giafly@sbcglobal.net	Nagpur	India	$12.00	2/2/2020	2
5	34053	Jonathan Black	jonathan@aol.com	Dongguan	China	$45.00	2/5/2020	2
6	34054	Louise Smith	louise@optonline.net	Havana	Cuba	$23.00	3/1/2020	3
7	34055	Seth Brown	sethbrown@yahoo.ca	Chicago	United States	$85.00	4/4/2020	2
8	34056	Randall Mcdonnell	rattenbt@yahoo.com	Vienna	Austria	$34.00	1/14/2020	1
9	34057	Mistie Vanhouten	aardo@live.com	Shenzen	China	$76.00	1/18/2020	4
10	34058	Lia Lacomb	bancboy@yahoo.com	İzmir	Turkey	$58.00	3/23/2020	1
11	34059	Leena Lande	pizza@gmail.com	Addis Ababa	Ethiopia	$24.00	2/28/2020	2
12	34060	Carleen Suits	ninenine@me.com	Seoul	South Korea	$39.00	3/18/2020	3
13	34061	Al Midgley	nichoj@me.com	Guayaquil	Ecuador	$20.00	3/29/2020	2
14	34062	Arletha Dagostino	fmtbebuck@live.com	Almaty	Kazakhstan	$93.00	1/29/2020	1
15	34063	Nancey Menz	baveja@outlook.com	Mandalay	Myanmar	$21.00	1/18/2020	3
16	34064	Agripina Fusco	grolschie@optonline.net	Fuzhou	China	$32.00	2/18/2020	4
17	34065	Tennie Pinzon	mrdvt@att.net	Calgary	Canada	$53.00	2/1/2020	3
18	34066	Nieves Hemstreet	csilvers@mac.com	Dar es Salaam	Tanzania	$26.00	1/25/2020	3
19	34067	Jewell Fullerton	cmdrgravy@verizon.net	Yokohama	Japan	$76.00	1/22/2020	3
20	34068	Connie Kroner	zilla@yahoo.com	Xiamen	China	$48.00	3/23/2020	1
21	34069	Pamelia Spurling	mwandel@sbcglobal.net	Córdoba	Argentina	$82.00	3/29/2020	3
22	34070	Veta Mulroy	yruan@aol.com	Taipei	Taiwan	$21.00	4/15/2020	4
23	34071	Nilda Chong	wilsonpm@comcast.net	Surat	India	$87.00	1/24/2020	4
24	34072	Ozie Wardlow	tarreau@optonline.net	Tehran	Iran	$12.00	2/19/2020	3

Figure 8.1 Basic customer records with behavioral data

of our marketing. From there, we can continue exploring other aspects of our data. For example, we could look at the following:

- Are there any patterns in demographics or behavioral data in the most profitable customers?
- Are there any patterns in the best performing marketing campaigns?
- Are there any issues in how we are attributing our users?

Customer Retention

These are the questions that we can answer using this workflow:

- What should be our ideal retention strategy?
- How long do we retain our customers?
- What behaviors contribute to long-term retention?

The data that will be needed here is as follows:

- List of all retained customers or users
- Demographic information about the users (name, e-mail, gender, location, etc.)

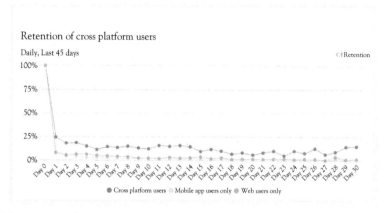

Figure 8.2 Slicing retention curves by segments[1]

- Behavioral information about the users (lifetime revenue, what products they use or purchased)
- 90 days of historical data

The key in this workflow is having enough demographic and behavioral information about our users. Once we have this, we can look at understanding how our best customers behave and interact with our business. Our initial answers can revolve around visualizing a retention curve where we can see overall retention drop over days, weeks, months, or years (Figure 8.2).

From there, we can start to segment our customer base to see if there are any attributes that seem to contribute to better retention. For example, we may discover that female users tend to be retained longer on average than male users.

We could also explore how different behaviors contribute to retention by converting them into segments. Instead of looking at female users, we could look at users who bought three products or more within the first 90 days of them becoming a customer.

---

[1] "Amplitude | Product Analytics for Web and Mobile." *Homepage, Amplitude*, https://amplitude.com/ (accessed May 7, 2020).

Process Performance

In this workflow, we want to understand how a given process is performing and how we could improve it. Common processes include sales, customer service, and operations. For our example, we'll use a sales process. The questions that we could answer are:

- Where are the prospects dropping in the sales process?
- What is the difference between the best and worst performing sales reps?
- How could we simplify the process and increase the speed in which sales close?

The data that will be needed here is as follows:

- List of prospects and won deals
- Demographic information about the users (name, e-mail, gender, location, etc.)
- Behavioral information about the prospects (their interest, touchpoints with sales reps, etc.)
- 180 days of historical data

You'll notice that I increase the historical data range here. This will vary depending on how long it takes for an average prospect to go through our sales process.

Since this is a sequential process, it will be helpful to have a visual representation of the steps in our process (Figure 8.3). This can be seen in a funnel or a pipeline where we can see conversion rates from each step to the next.

We want to understand where the biggest drop-offs are happening and what steps take a long time to complete. It would be helpful to also see if these conversions rate change by segments. We could look at expected deal size, source of deal, sales rep, and much more.

The next step is to understand how won deals are different from lost deals. Do they have more touchpoints? Do they close faster or slower? Are there specific attributes that seem to be more likely to close?

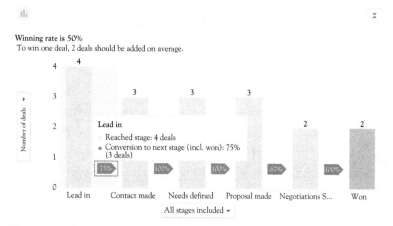

Figure 8.3 Visualizing a funnel or process to spot drop-offs[2]

It's important to understand that we want to improve the overall process. You may discover that one of your sales reps needs coaching and that's important. However, helping a single sales rep might not have a big enough impact on the process. Focus on making things move as smoothly as possible.

Customer Success Performance

In this workflow, we want to understand who our best customers are and how well are we serving them. The questions that we could answer are:

- How do our best customers interact with our company?
- Who are the least profitable or highest time-consuming customers?
- How effective are we at helping our customers when they have issues or questions?

The data that will be needed here is as follows:

- List of active customers
- Demographic information about the users (name, e-mail, gender, location, etc.)

---

[2] "Sales CRM & Pipeline Management Software | Pipedrive." *Homepage*, Pipedrive, https://pipedrive.com/ (accessed January 1, 2020).

- Behavioral information about the customers (purchase history, interactions with customer support, etc.)
- 180 days of historical data

Let's start by getting high-level numbers on how our customers engage with our company. How often do they purchase from us? How often do they get in touch with customer support? What is their lifetime value (LTV) and cost to acquire?

We then want to analyze how the bottom and top 10 percent differ. What is the difference in LTV? What is the difference in purchase history? Do they get in touch less or more?

Finally, we want to understand how well we support our customers in general. We'll need to dive deep into customer support metrics to look at the average response time, percent of successful closed cases, customer feedback, and more. It's important to also separate the best customers from the worst customers in this analysis. There's only so much we can do for some customers.

Qualitative Data Analysis

In this workflow, we want to understand how our customers feel about our company and products. We will be focusing on qualitative data such as surveys, interviews, and digital usage.

- How likely are customers to recommend our products and services?
- How are customers engaging with our digital products?
- Are there any potential products or services that we could launch or tweak to better serve customers?

The data that will be needed here is as follows:

- Surveys, interviews, website heatmaps, or other qualitative data
- Matching customer data showing demographic and behavioral characteristics
- 90 days of historical data

Qualitative data can be tricky to analyze but we can add a few things that can make it easier to work with. To start, we can use scoring systems that can convert customer feedback into quantitative numbers. An example would be the Net Promoter Score (NPS) which measures how likely someone is to recommend our products and services on a scale of 1 to 10. We could then group or rank our users based on their scores.

We can also go through the customer responses and look for keywords within their responses. This can be used to find patterns of concerns or ideas for future products.

We can also tie all of this data into their customer data to gauge the importance of feedback. Not every customer is the same and we can go down rabbit holes trying to help unprofitable customers.

Regardless of which workflow that you use or if you come up with your own, the principles are the same. In the next section, we will talk about how to automatically surface these insights to reduce manual labor and increase the speed at which your team learns. For more resources on data analysis and workflows, please visit datamiragebook.com.

How to Automatically Surface Insights

Thanks to technology, the process of data analysis is becoming increasingly easier. This is where machine learning and AI can come in but there are a few things you can do to automatically surface insights. Let's look at these options and how they could help reduce the overall time spent analyzing data.

Establish a Regular Cadence for Interacting with the Data

The first thing that you need is the ability to automatically send data in the form of reports and dashboards. This data should be refreshed on its own and should be sent in multiple formats. Some people prefer to receive this in e-mail format, others want to get a link that could click through, and others might want to see it inside their team chat tools like Slack and Microsoft Teams.

The goal here is to make it easy for people to interact with the data and notice any trends or changes in their KPIs. They may see a spike or they may see something within the latest report that warrants further analysis or an experiment. Simply getting people to use the data on a consistent basis in a way that doesn't take up a lot of their time is valuable.

Monitor Anomalies and Opportunities

The second thing you could do is to monitor anomalies and opportunities. Once you have some historical data, you'll be able to know when the numbers change in a significant way. This may mean that a certain KPI increased or decreased by 15 percent more than the average.

This is what we would call an anomaly or opportunity. A spike could be an increase in traffic or sales and a drop could be a technical issue or error. Either way, you want to have a system that can notice these anomalies and automatically notify the right people. Without this system, you'll need to wait until people find them which could be a few days or a couple of weeks.

Use Machine Learning for Finding Insights

The third thing you could do is to use machine learning to find insights. This will require the support of a data scientist but this can be a great way to take your data and run it through some unsupervised learning to surface any patterns or insights. You could eventually even automate this process altogether and send the results by e-mail or another format. I'll cover this idea in more detail in our machine learning chapter later on in this book.

Regardless of how you analyze your data, this is a crucial step that everyone in your team should understand. Some people will be more proficient while others will be more limited in what they are able to do. Regardless of their ability, it's important that everyone understands how to take insights and convert them into experiments. This is what we will discuss in our next chapter.

Chapter Summary

- There's a process to data analysis that anyone can learn; however, this process takes time.
- You need to have a solid understanding of your KPIs, your customers, and human behavior in general.
- Start by determining what questions you would like to answer, gather all the relevant data, get basic answers, play with the data to work through assumptions, and finish by coming up with conclusions.
- Every analysis workflow has a series of common attributes that could be applied to any business.
- Automatically surface insights by establishing routines for looking at data, monitoring anomalies, and using machine learning.

CHAPTER 9

Building Experiments and Making Better Decisions

It is common sense to take a method and try it. If it fails, admit it frankly and try another. But above all, try something.
—Franklin D. Roosevelt (*Looking Forward*)

There's something special about finding insights. You realized that 50 percent of your customers came from a specific campaign. Perhaps you realized that you're able to acquire customers from less than they are worth to you, allowing you to scale your campaigns. Each of these insights has a level of energy or electricity when they are first shared.

And yet, insights without action are just mental entertainment. Insights by themselves don't turn themselves into top-line or bottom-line growth. They don't help you reduce costs or retain your best talent. You need to do something about these insights. You need to take action.

In this chapter, we will look at how insights can be converted into experiments and better decisions. The word experiments might take you back to science class and dissecting frogs but almost everything that a company does can be seen as an experiment. You're not sure if a new product will do well or if a new marketing campaign will resonate until you launch it. Once you see the initial data, you can adjust toward success.

This process doesn't have to be random. We can design frameworks under which we test ideas, refine them, and convert them into tangible results. This same framework can help us make better decisions over the long term. This doesn't mean that every decision will be the right one but in aggregate, we will be in the black.

Let's start by looking at one of my favorite questions: What Does It Mean (WDIM)?

Why Turn Insights into Experiments and WDIM

Insights are fantastic. Most companies would be excited if they could be uncovering interesting insights about their customers and products. However, insights are still one step removed from what really matters— answering the "What Does It Mean" question. This question is our ultimate goal.

The WDIM question is the hardest to answer because it isn't just objective facts. An objective fact is that it will rain tomorrow. The WDIM answer is that you should bring an umbrella and wear your favorite rain jacket. Insights tell you what happened but WDIM tells you why you should care.

There are two reasons why companies struggle with the WDIM question. First, there's a disconnect between business teams and technical teams. Second, WDIM answers carry consequences. Let's explore each one in detail.

Our data lives within the context of the business. Any insights are meant to help the business grow. We can therefore reason that we need to analyze the data within the constraints of business theory. How will this help our sales? Will this affect our cash position? Can we sustain this over the long term?

These are the "business" questions that we need to answer. The disconnect comes from how data is collected and visualized. The requests from data come from business folks but they are typically managed by technical folks. This can lead to reports and dashboards that are fantastic but aren't able to fully answer all the business questions we care about.

This forces executives to come up with their conclusions as to what they should do. However, the closer we can get to the WDIM question, the more valuable the data is. Companies can solve this first challenge in two ways. One way involves hiring more business-minded technical folks. Another way involves improving communication between these two groups of people.

The second reason why companies struggle with WDIM is because of consequences. Consequences, you ask? This isn't a life or death situation. I'm not talking about life or death consequences but livelihood ones. Let's look at an example to see what I mean.

Let's imagine that we came across an insight that sales are dropping for our best selling product. We can see the trend over two quarters. This is in the insight, backed by data. An objective fact is you will. The WDIM answer is that we need to update the product and how we market it. We'll need to launch new marketing campaigns and do some R&D on the product itself.

The consequences of the WDIM answer are that we will need to spend significant money and time working on this product. After all this, we may still fail to reverse this trend. If it fails, what happens? Does someone get the blame? Will someone get fired? These are the consequences.

Executives naturally have to deal with consequences because that's their job. But what about the data analyst? Or the director of marketing? How high up do you have to go until the WDIM question makes sense for your role?

Ideally, everyone would be incentivized to work on the WDIM question. You could then compare notes and make the best decision. This is what companies talk about when it comes to giving more ownership to their employees.

Decisions require courage because you may be wrong. Ironically, the best way to get closer to the RIGHT decision is through trial and error. This is one of the main concepts from Nassim Taleb who has written books like *The Black Swan* and *Skin in the Game*. This is how he describes it:

> *The knowledge we get by tinkering, via trial and error, experience, and the workings of time, in other words, contact with the earth, is vastly superior to that obtained through reasoning, something self-serving institutions have been very busy hiding from us.*
> —Nassim Nicholas Taleb, *Skin in the Game:*
> *Hidden Asymmetries in Daily Life*

This is what brings us to experiments. An experiment is the act of trying to validate (or invalidate) a hypothesis that you may have. Perhaps you're trying to improve the sales of a failing product or you're trying to launch a brand new product. Experiments let us take our WDIM answers and test them.

If we are wrong, we can run another experiment. This trial-and-error process is better than the original design. We can't foresee all the challenges that will come up but we could iterate through solutions rapidly.

Experiments also remove the pressure from WDIM questions. We move away from the idea of limited shots and embrace moving quickly. We strive toward "good enough" in our decisions and then take action. Our data doesn't have to be perfect and flawless. Our insights don't have to be earth shattering.

Let's now look at how we can build our own experimentation framework. This could be done companywide or teamwide.

Building a Framework for Data-Driven Decisions and Experiments

Running experiments sounds easy. Think of an idea, design the experiment, and then see how it performs. While this may result in random wins, it will not lead to long-term growth. Instead, we want to approach this in a systematic and scientific way. This is where frameworks come in.

A framework is a process in which you take ideas through to validate them, test them, and iterate on them. While processes may seem bureaucratic, they are designed to remove mistakes. Mistakes are what can derail an entire experiment. You'll quickly see how easy it is to make a mistake when designing experiments.

All frameworks are built on the following elements:

1. Idea capture
2. Prioritization
3. Experiment design
4. Measurement
5. Learning

Let's look at each element in detail.

Idea Capture

This is where you will capture all the potential ideas that you could be testing. Get everyone in your team (or company) to contribute to get a wide spread of possibilities. If you have ever struggled to implement the plethora of ideas that you come across in blog posts, conferences, podcasts, and conversations, this is for you. Don't complicate this. It can be as simple as a spreadsheet capturing the essence of the idea.

Prioritization

The real magic in the process happens here. You'll always have too many ideas and you need to prioritize. Your criteria should be objective. I constantly come across companies who are swayed by random criteria. Maybe the idea came from the CEO or a competitor started doing something similar. Objectivity will make it easier to judge and improve over the long term.

Your criteria should encompass the different variables of the experiment such as:

- Potential impact on KPIs
- Cost to implement/design
- Alignment with strategy
- Likelihood of success

Over time, you'll add new criteria. However, you can get started with three to five ideas right away. Even a simple framework like ICE (Impact, Confidence, Ease of Implementation) is enough in the beginning.

Experiment Design

This format design of your experiment will be straightforward. You simply design the experiment which could be a change to your website/product, updated copy, new features, and so on. The next section will look at the most common types of experiments and how to use them.

Instead, I want to focus on the statistical numbers behind experiments. You need to know if the results of an experiment are statistically significant. This is a fancy way of saying that the results are valid and aren't simply random. Software tools can give you this number but preplan the overall test.

It's helpful to use a pretest calculator to project how long it will take to see results and how much traffic is needed. Figure 9.1 is one of my favorites from a site called CXL:

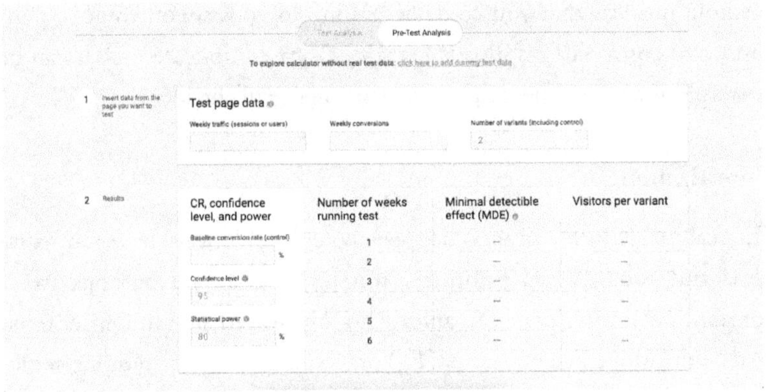

Figure 9.1 An example of a pretest calculator from CXL[1]

You'll need to consider how much traffic will be sent to this experiment, how many variants you're using, and what the baseline conversion rate is. Based on that, you'll have an idea of how much change you can detect within the first few weeks.

In Figure 9.1, we can see that the "Minimal Detectable Effect (MDE)" on Week 2 is 139.00 percent. This means that for a variation to be more successful, it needs to be 139.00 percent better than the baseline or around 13.9 percent in conversion rate. It also tells us how much traffic should have hit each variant.

We'll talk about how to analyze experiments after they are done but you want to make sure that you aren't ending experiments prematurely.

Measurement

If you have done the previous steps in this book and in this chapter, then measurement should be a breeze. Fundamentally, you want to track how each variant of your test converts. The conversion should be something tangible like a purchase or user sign-up though you could have multiple conversions. How you track this will depend on your testing software and how well structured your data is.

---

[1] "AB Test Sample Size Calculators by CXL." *Homepage, CXL*, https://cxl.com/ab-test-calculator/ (accessed on January 1, 2020).

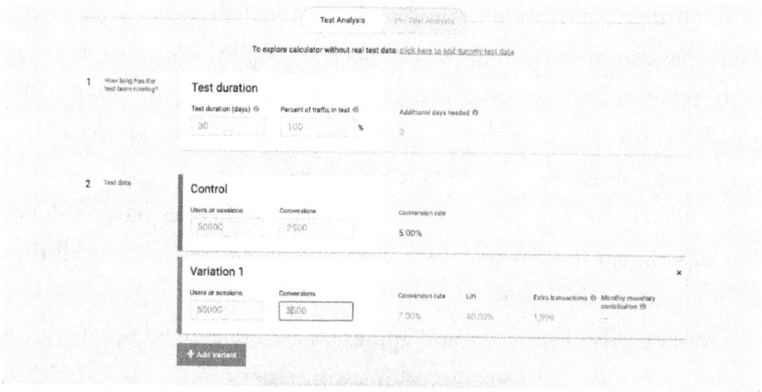

Figure 9.2 An example of a posttest calculator from CXL[2]

Learning

Once a test is done, you need to analyze it. This means looking through the final numbers to determine if your variant performs better than the baseline. We can go back to the calculator we saw earlier (Figure 9.2).

You can see what kind of lift you got (if any). Running through the pretest analysis means there should be few surprises here. This kind of calculator can break through any assumptions about "winners." It's not just the conversion rate that matters. We need to see how it compares within a statistical context. Lucky for us, we don't need to learn complex statistics.

Regardless of the outcome of your test, you will learn something. Winning variations feel great but "failed" experiments also teach us something. Have a process for capturing these insights. Here are a few questions to ask.

- How did the experiment compare against our initial assumptions?
- What surprised us the most?
- How could have this experiment been performed differently?
- How has the result of this experiment changed our upcoming experiments?
- What else don't we know?

---

[2] "AB Test Sample Size Calculators by CXL." *Homepage, CXL,* https://cxl.com/ab-test-calculator (accessed January 1, 2020).

You'll then repeat the entire process and launch a new experiment. The magic here is in your ability to iterate through this process in a consistent fashion. Sticking to the process matters here, so keep it simple. You can add complexity over the long run. For more information on testing frameworks, please visit datamiragebook.com.

I'll now show you how some of the best companies have designed their experiment frameworks. Let's start by looking at one of my all-time favorite companies, Spotify.

I love Spotify. This is a music app that's available on all devices. I use Spotify every day and usually multiple times per day. I also think their product is quite good and they happened to also share the inner workings of their company.

Spotify created a framework they called DIBB or Data-Insight-Belief-Bet.[2] This is their way of taking insights and converting them into experiments which they call bets (Figure 9.3).

The second framework that we can study is one from Facebook. Now Facebook is a large company and their teams might use different

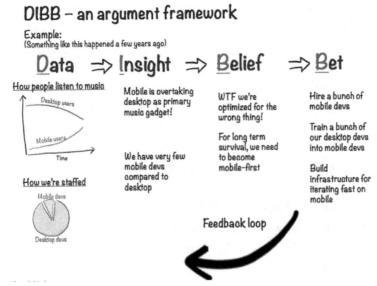

Figure 9.3 Spotify's DIBB framework

---

2   https://blog.crisp.se/2016/06/08/henrikkniberg/spotify-rhythm

frameworks. We'll focus on the one used by the Messenger team which they have called EVELYN.

This framework stands for Experiment Velocity Engine (Lifting Your Numbers). I'll let Darius Contractor, the person who created this while working at Dropbox and Facebook, explain it:

> The idea is it's pretty much an experiment tracker, an organizing tool that allows you to put in all your experiments, prioritize them well, track them from specing, designing, building and completion and also see how you did, like opportunity sizing on the way in, look at the results on the way out, and overall give you a set of processes and a storage source of truth for your experiments that I think can really help a team accelerate how they build and build the right experiments, getting you to more growth wins faster.[3]

Your framework doesn't have to be as complex as Spotify's or Facebook's but you do need one. This is how you can make the most out of the insights that will arise from your data. Let's now look at the different formats for running experiments.

Measure Experiments through Data

While every company will run different experiments, everyone is using the same formats. I wanted to explore each one in more detail so you understand how it works and how to track it.

A/B Testing Websites and Apps

A/B testing allows you to test two (or more) variations of the same idea. This could be landing pages, website pop-ups, or call to actions. Using the right tools, we can see if an idea performs better than the average using statistical models. You don't need to learn the math behind these models

---

[3] "This Framework from Facebook's Darius Contractor Is the Secret to Faster Growth | Drift." *Homepage*, Drift, last modified June 26, 2019, https://www. drift.com/blog/secret-to-faster-growth/

as the tools will calculate them for you. You can also preplan your tests as shown in the section above.

Messaging

The second type of experiment that you could run is on the messages that you're sending users. For most companies, this might be e-mail but it could also include push notifications, in-app notifications, and SMS.

Your experiments could include testing two messages against each (A/B test format) or you could test the overall framework in which you're sending the messages. You can track the performance of your messages by designing funnels that have a short conversion window, for example, one hour to get a sense of how any given message drives action.

Copy

The third type of experiment would be around copy. We can focus on the copy of a website or app for this category. Words matter and they are one of the areas in which you could see significant improvements to your performance. You can use reports like heatmaps and conversion funnels to understand if your copy is performing as expected.

Feature Adoption

The fourth type of experiment revolves around product features. When you release a new feature, you'll want to see if this is being adopted by your users as you hoped. You can analyze methods like cohort analysis and user retention to understand this experiment.

Using Machine Learning

I also wanted to make a note on how machine learning could help you measure your experiments. We'll cover machine learning and data science in more detail in Chapter 10 but it's relevant for this section. The "Impact" report we saw earlier is actually using simple machine learning models to understand the adoption of a feature.

These machine learning-powered reports can be a great way to add more advanced analysis techniques into your team on a regular basis. You can look for them as you select tools and vendors.

A Crash Course on Correlation Versus Causation

All teams will discover patterns in how their users are engaging with their products but they will be unsure if a user doing a certain action is causing something else or if they are merely correlated.

If you're falling asleep, I don't blame you. This likely feels like a throwback to college or university; however, I'll do my best to break this down into simple terms and actions that your team can use right away.

Let's start by understanding what these two words even mean!

Don't Fall Asleep: Causation and Correlation in Simple Terms

Causation simply means that X was responsible for Y. Ice cream sales go up in the summer and we can safely say that hot weather causes this increase. On the other hand, we may have two actions that seem to have a relationship but aren't necessarily caused by each other. These two actions are correlated but may lack causation (Figure 9.4).

We may see a decrease in ice cream sales around the start of the year due to New Year resolutions. Causation is unclear but there seems to be a relationship. Perhaps people are tired of sweets from the holidays or the weather starts to turn cold around January.

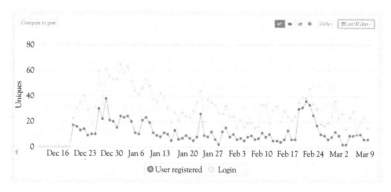

Figure 9.4 Trend of two variables over time

You'll also notice that the relationship could be positive (both variables increase or decrease together) or negative (one variable increases while the other decreases) or there could be no relationship at all (increases or decreases are random).

For advanced product teams, it's important to understand these two terms and how they might play out within their product. You may realize that users who sign up using their Facebook account have higher retention rates than those who simply use their e-mail address. Or you may notice a significant change to your north star metric.

This insight could then lead you to force every user to sign up via Facebook which could lead to plummeting retention rates over the long term. Assuming that something is the cause can be disastrous without double-checking your assumptions.

There are no easy answers when it comes to separating actions that seem to be correlated from those that are truly connected to each other (causation). For every hypothesis that you have, you'll need to run it through a battery of tests to prove or disprove it.

Correlation and Causation from the Real World

Besides the ice cream example, let's use a few other examples that companies are likely to run into.

Situation #1: Product Redesign

Let's imagine that your team has decided to redesign your product or website. After you launch the redesign, you notice a sharp increase in user engagement or traffic to your website. Is the redesign the cause of this increase?

They are likely correlated but causation will be hard to prove. Traffic increase could have come from a different source and even user engagement could be caused by another source like communication journeys.

This is also a great example of something that might be hard to prove because redesign doesn't happen often. This means that it will be hard to duplicate the scenario in an A/B test but you could test the other elements such as new onboarding flows or new marketing campaigns.

Situation #2: New Onboarding Flow

In this example, your team is getting ready to release a new onboarding flow that should make it easier for users to start using your product. The new onboarding flow converts at a higher rate than the old one.

In this case, causation is likely to be found because we are looking at a very specific part of the product. Better yet, we can easily test this by A/B testing the new flow versus the old one on random groups of users.

Situation #3: New Cultural Values

Let's now look at a trickier example. Let's imagine that your company goes through a company retreat and ends up adopting new values for your organization. You then notice that all your core KPIs increase over the following 90 days.

Causation versus correlation will be hard to prove in this scenario because of how separated the actions are (new cultural values and KPIs increasing). However, over time, you could disqualify other factors and if the increases stick, you could at least attribute correlation.

The common themes through these scenarios and many others are as follows:

- The more complex the situation, the harder it is to prove correlation, let alone causation.
- Highly specific situations, for example, onboarding flows, can be easily tested through randomized A/B tests to get statistical significance.
- It takes times to prove or disprove any situation so you need to consider if this is something that is important to your team.

Strategies for Getting the Right Answer

As mentioned in the previous section, there are three different ways to test for causation versus correlation in the real world. Let's look at each one and where you would use them.

A/B Tests

The best option here is to run properly designed A/B tests. The keyword here is "properly." The test should randomize who sees specific variations (or flows), get enough volume to reach statistical significance, and run the tests for long enough to see short-term business cycles.

It isn't enough to just run the test and make a decision with whatever data you have. You will also need to run multiple tests confirming the same hypothesis. In the onboarding example above, this might include the following tests:

- Existing versus existing onboarding flow (calibrate your tool)
- New versus existing onboarding flow
- New versus existing flows for specific segments:
    - Web desktop-only traffic
    - Mobile traffic only
- Cohort analysis of the new versus existing group of users over time

Further Analysis

A second option is to dive deeper into the data to prove or disprove a hypothesis. Assuming you have the data, you would be focused on finding the correct user segments and behaviors. Let's imagine that you're trying to understand how a specific feature is affecting your overall retention rate. Using your existing data, you would do the following analysis:

- Cohort analysis of users who used the feature versus those who didn't
- Average user engagement of feature
- Analyzing individual users who engage with the feature
- Surveying users who engage with future versus those who didn't

Ignoring It

The third option is to ignore it altogether. This may sound crazy (or lazy) but there are situations that aren't worth the effort to analyze them.

A perfect example is a product redesign. This is something that doesn't have very often and isn't easy to test using A/B tests. You could use "Further Analysis" but the question becomes: what's the point?

If you do realize that the redesign helped, are you going to run another redesign? Unlikely. If you realize that the redesign didn't help, are you going to roll back? Maybe, depending on how much a team likes a new redesign and the impact.

This isn't to say that you shouldn't analyze the performance of a redesign but that shouldn't worry too much about the causation versus correlation question.

Regardless of which option you choose, they take time and resources. This is like trying to put together a puzzle. Every test or analysis will add one more piece to the overall design but it will take multiple pieces before you can see the overall picture.

Bonus Points: The Humor Behind Correlation Versus Causation

Now that we went through all the serious stuff, let's take a moment and look at the humor behind this. If you look hard enough, you can find a correlation almost anywhere.

To prove this, I spent a few minutes doing this for public data sets. I used the hilarious site created by Tyler Vigen[4] where he has created a tool to easily correlate a wide array of variables.

Take all the charts (Figures 9.5, 9.6, and 9.7) given here with a grain of salt and enjoy the silliness.

The first example is people who literally worked themselves to death and the sales of General Mills cereals.

It seems that the more you eat cereal, the more likely you are to work yourself to death.

Next, we have the divorce rates in Alabama and the per capita consumption of whole milk.

Lucky for us, it seems that as people drink less milk, the divorce rate goes down. Or perhaps the consumption of milk goes down as people

---

[4] "Spurious Correlations," *Homepage.* Tyler Vigen, last modified January 1, 2020, https://tylervigen.com/spurious-correlations.

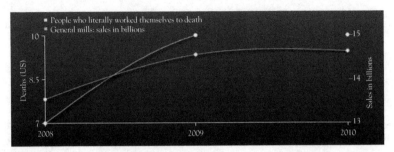

Figure 9.5 Does eating General Mills cereal lead to death? Unlikely

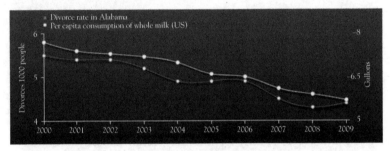

Figure 9.6 To decrease divorces, Alabama should focus on increasing milk consumption, according to this chart

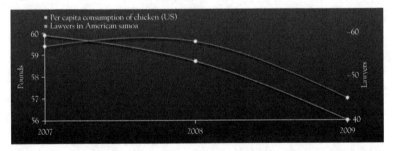

Figure 9.7 Lower consumption of chicken is leading to fewer lawyers in Samoa

get divorced less. Either way, if you want to avoid getting divorced in Alabama, drink less milk.

Finally, we have the per capita consumption of chicken and the number of lawyers in American Samoa.

Just like before, the fewer lawyers in American Samoa, the less the United States consumes chicken. The chicken industry should clearly be investing billions of dollars into law schools in American Samoa.

Let's come back to the serious stuff. Remember that correlation and causation are advanced topics when it comes to product analysis. In almost all examples, the more data is always better and the better structured you are at running experiments, the more likely you are to find answers (either proving or disproving your hypothesis).

Chapter Summary

- Answering the WDIM question is hard but that's where the value lies.
- Trial and error will allow you to find the "right" answer much quicker than just thinking through things.
- Experiment frameworks have five elements: idea capture, prioritization, experiment design, measurement, learning.
- The key to these frameworks is the ability to run through them consistently and on a regular cadence.
- You can measure your experiments through data in different forms and reports.
- Correlation versus causation is hard but even a basic understanding of it will help you make better decisions.

CHAPTER 10

Beyond the Basics: Machine Learning, AI, and the Future

"Siri, what's the weather in San Francisco?" I still remember the first time I used Siri. It seems quite magical, which is something that has happened quite often with Apple products. Back in 2011, Siri had a slight lag but it was still incredible. You could use your voice and get someone (or something) to respond back to you with relevant answers.

Despite the obvious limitations of Siri, it was a great showcase of the power of machine learning and what would become data science. The study of how computers think dates back all the way to the 1950s but it would take a long time before we could see its fruits in such obvious ways like Siri.

Siri also came at a time when AI and machine learning were starting to become mainstream. We didn't know it back then but it would go on to be critical to many of the technological developments of the last few years. Being able to process large amounts of data to predict the future would be a game changer.

A year later, the *Harvard Business Review* called data scientists the "sexiest job of the 21st Century."[1] This drove an increase in interest and people training to become data scientists. In this chapter, I'll show you the basics of data science and how your company should think about it from a business perspective. This isn't a technical look at machine learning but a strategic one.

---

[1] "Data Scientist: The Sexiest Job of the 21st Century." Blog Post, *Harvard Business Review*, https://hbr.org/2012/10/data-scientist-the-sexiest-job-of-the-21st-century (accessed on October 1, 2012).

Fundamentals Will Get You Far

The world of data science is sexy and new. The possibilities seem endless. I also think that there's a significant value that can be created through machine learning and AI. However, I also think that the fundamentals will get you quite far.

It can be tempting to jump into data science right away. The reality is that you need to have your basics in place before you ever attempt any data science projects. I constantly see this need to jump ahead. To want to be in the advanced field right away. I think there are several reasons for this.

First, companies don't always have the resources or time to wait for answers. Machine learning can seem like a way to get insights quicker. If you can input your data into a model and get insights, why wouldn't you do that? We actually spoke about this in Chapter 8 when we talked about surfacing insights automatically. The ideas that I covered then didn't actually require machine learning. You just needed the right tools or data structure.

Nonetheless, there is a rise in "automated machine learning." Tools that will surface insights or they will find outliers in your data using simple models. This is helpful but don't rely on it as your primary way of analyzing data. Your company needs to be able to go through your data and understand it.

The second reason why companies want to prematurely skip ahead to machine learning is because they believe their problems are complex. If you're struggling with growth, bad retention, or retaining employees, there could be temptation to gravitate toward complex solutions, for example, models. This may be the case but you may also just need another solution. Take the people issues that we covered throughout this book. You could conclude that instead of managing expectations and training people, you could simply let machines do all the analysis. This approach is less likely to work because you haven't actually solved the underlying problem.

The third reason why companies jump into data science too early is because there is a tangible value there. The use cases I'll cover later on in this chapter are real. For some businesses, we are talking about a

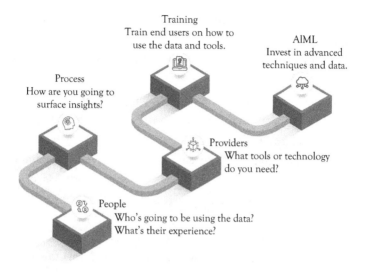

Figure 10.1 Data-supported culture

significant revenue increase or cost savings. It can be hard to ignore that because you "don't have the basics covered." Why can't just work on this and tackle the basics later?

When I work with companies, I always talk about having a data-supported culture. This is slightly different from a data-driven culture, which I don't think is the right fit for most companies. In this type of culture, the basics are all the things that come before data science. In Figure 10.1, it's steps 1 to 4. These aren't just nice to have; they are pre-requisites to data science.

Let's now talk about what exactly data science is. This is a fast-changing field with a lot of hype but we can uncover the truth.

Data Science Terms to Know

Before we move on to the next section, let's define a few terms to get on the same page. This isn't an exhaustive list but they are the most popular terms that you're bound to come across.

Machine Learning = use of algorithms to understand data and then make predictions

Algorithms = set of instructions to process data

Artificial Intelligence (AI) = field exploring how machines can be self-aware

Deep Learning = a machine learning model to classify data, for example, facial recognition

Data Science = answering questions about the future

Data Analysis = answering questions about the present and past

Data Engineering = building the systems that capture and store data

Business Intelligence (BI) = focus on creating reports and dashboards

What Is Data Science?

Data science to me is about the future. Plain and simple. We are interested in understanding what the future may hold and how to respond to it. In comparison, data analysis is focused on the present and past. The bulk of this book has focused on helping you understand what is going on right now. The fundamentals are all about the present and past.

The reason why you need the fundamentals before you get into data science is simple. To understand the future, we need to know where we come from—what happened in the past which might give us a clue as to what might happen in the future. If we can't understand what is going on right now, it will be extremely difficult to predict the future.

One of the most common techniques used in data science to understand the future is machine learning. This is where you used algorithms to process data and make predictions. Self-driving cars are a grand example of this. The car (or software) is collecting all this input such as weather conditions, other cars, road signs, and pedestrians. Based on this data, it then makes predictions on how fast the car should move, when to stop, and when to turn. It's not just one prediction but thousands and millions of them.

A more simplified example would be a machine learning model that can detect cat pictures. We started by feeding the model a whole bunch of cat pictures. The model will start to detect patterns in how cats typically look. They might have tails and fur and be of a certain size. Eventually, we could give it a brand new photo it has never seen before and determine if it's a cat or not. We are processing data and eventually making predictions about the future which we have not seen.

As you can quickly see, data is quite important to this process. It's not just any data. We need the right data and lots of it. We then need to train models by feeding them this data and optimize how it responds. While it may seem like machine learning models are completely self-sufficient, they actually need quite a bit of training. One of the major challenges for companies is having enough resources to handle this training.

Let's now jump into the most practical use case of data science and how you could use it at your company.

Practical Use Cases of Data Science

Despite the hype and the never-ending "AI startups," there are significant use cases of data science. I will organize them into four broad categories. You may have others but these are mine. I don't expect that all four categories will apply to your business but they can start to give you ideas as to what your company could do. In the next section, I'll cover the prerequisites to data science so you're able to determine if this is worthwhile for your company.

Fraud Detection

The first category is dealing with fraud. This is especially helpful for companies in the banking, payment processing, and cryptocurrency industries. Machine learning models can be deployed to determine "fraud flags" which could then be applied proactively to new transactions. Remember, it's not enough to just understand the past. We need to make predictions about the future for this to be considered data science.

A great example of this category would be the Radar product by Stripe. Stripe is a payment processing company and they are able to take the billions of transactions that flow through their network to train their models. Based on this, they have developed thousands of signals which they then convert into a fraud score. If the rating is too high, they can automatically block the transaction. Otherwise, they can give the merchant an option to block it.

What I love about this model is that most of the work is hidden. You'll see this pattern repeat over and over again. The output of this model might seem quite small. It's just a score or it's an automated flagging of a transaction. However, underneath this "simple" output, there's significant data that is being processed and dissected.

Recommendations

The second category helps companies make better recommendations. Netflix and Amazon will come to mind right away. Netflix is trying to make movie recommendations based on your taste. They have actually developed more than 2,000 taste groups,[2] which then determine what movies you might see on your screen.

It used to be that recommendations were made simply on similar categories or tags. Netflix has expanded to include behavioral information on what you're watching now and in the past. Once again, we are analyzing the past and present and then making a future prediction to the user.

Another example of this type of model would be StitchFix. They offer clothing recommendations at scale and they have used machine learning models to determine what clothes should be recommended to each user.[3] They identified hundreds of preferences and then sort through the data to figure out what users might like. This model doesn't work on its own. It's actually paired up with humans to get a holistic picture.

Cost Reduction

The third practical use case of data science is the ability to reduce costs using models. This is similar to fraud detection but that use case deserves its own category. A common example of cost reduction is the use of algorithms to optimize how you spend marketing dollars. Most companies use attribution models to determine what channels should get more

---

[2] "This is how Netflix's top-secret recommendation system works." Blog Post, Wired, last modified, https://wired.co.uk/article/how-do-netflixs-algorithms-work-machine-learning-helps-to-predict-what-viewers-will-like (accessed on August 22, 2012).
[3] "Stitch Fix's CEO on Selling Personal Style to the Mass Market." Blog Post, Harvard Business Review, https://hbr.org/2018/05/stitch-fixs-ceo-on-selling-personal-style-to-the-mass-market (accessed on May 01, 2012).

dollars. This is where terms like "last touch attribution" and "first touch attribution" come from.

Companies can adopt a "multichannel attribution" model which looks at all the channels that played a role in acquiring a customer. However, this is more art than science. You won't get clear-cut answers and instead, you'll need to make assumptions and then test them.

Algorithm-driven attribution tries to remove the uncertainty by using machine learning to figure out the best allocation of dollars. These models take into account different variables and determine the probability of the user converting with any given combination of channels. While this requires lots of data, it can be a good way to optimize your marketing campaigns.

Innovation

The fourth category relates to innovation. This is typically what people think when data science comes up in conversation. Prominent examples include self-driving cars and Alexa. In this category, machine learning isn't supporting something but is critical to the delivery of that product.

If we take the self-driving car example, this wouldn't be possible without machine learning. The product needs to capture all the different road conditions, analyze them, and then make a prediction for how the car should react. The same logic applies to assistants like Alexa, Google Assistant, and Siri. They take voice recordings, process them, and then determine the best response for that voice input.

Regardless of the practical use that is better suited for your company, we need certain prerequisites to make them. I refer to them as the "right data, right people, and right projects."

The Right Data, Right People, Right Projects

Before you tackle a data science project, we need to ensure that you're ready for this endeavor. Whenever a client approaches me about this kind of work, I'm looking for three things that will increase the chances of success.

Right Data

Having the right data goes beyond the fundamentals that we spoke about earlier. You don't want to waste time trying to hunt down data and clean it. This is what is called "data preparation" and it is estimated that data scientists spend between 60 and 80 percent simply organizing their data.[4] I can't guarantee that this will go down to 0 percent but you can significantly reduce that work needed here.

In a way, this entire book is designed to organize your data so it is easier to analyze and mine for insights. Having the right data means keeping a consistent data schema that is accurate and makes sense. It also means that you have managed to centralize your data in a data warehouse or data lake and this is being automatically updated.

You also need to make sure that you're able to solve the "people" issues that we have covered throughout this book. Building trust in the data, dealing with funky data, and working through psychological biases—if you're able to do all this, you'll be in a fantastic place to run advanced projects on your data.

Right People

After the right data, you need to have the right people. We have covered roles briefly in this book and data science projects require you to have the right people. While I'm a big believer in training internal talent and nurturing "hidden unicorn talent," this only goes so far with data science.

By its very nature, you will need certain skill sets that are hard to train internally. These are typically skills that get taught in academic settings and refined through real-life work. Skills like advanced statistics, computational math, and model design aren't easy skills.

This also explains why there's a shortage of qualified data scientists going around. Keep in mind that I'm talking about PhD-backed data

---

[4] "Cleaning Big Data: Most Time-Consuming, Least Enjoyable Data Science Task, Survey Says." Blog Post, *Forbes*, https://forbes.com/sites/gilpress/2016/03/23/data-preparation-most-time-consuming-least-enjoyable-data-science-task-survey-says/#182ae8996f63 (accessed on March 23, 2012).

scientists here who would be capable of working on complex projects and ideas. I think some companies are hiring entry-level data scientists and using them as data analysts but that's a different topic. Learn common mistakes companies make when hiring data scientists and data analysts by visiting datamiragebook.com.

Right Projects

Finally, you need to have the right projects. This may seem obvious but data science is hard. It takes a long time (months to years) and it requires significant resources. If you're going through all this effort, work on worthwhile things.

When choosing a project, you want to work on things that could provide a significant impact on the bottom line, help establish a differentiator (or moat) or something that will reduce operations costs. It should also be something that you can't do without machine learning.

It's important to ensure that you're not using data science as a hammer and seeing everything as a nail. This will be the most expensive hammer you will ever buy so you need to use it wisely.

Conclusion

There's a local telecom company here in Canada that has one of my favorite slogans. It is "The Future Is Friendly."[5] This is how I hope you feel about your data and company right now. I started this book by talking about the misconceptions that companies have when it comes to data and ensuring that you're playing the right game. I want to finish it by reminding you about the possibilities.

Data can infuse new life into a company or project. Data can reduce the uncertainty and frustration that we all go through in our work. Data can uncover things that you had never even thought about. Data can be a competitive advantage.

---

[5] "Phones, Internet and TV on Canada's fastest network | TELUS." *Homepage*, Telus, last modified January 1, 2020, https://www.telus.com/en/

My hope is that you use the ideas in this book to get more value out of your data. This will look different for every company but there's something in here for everyone.

The future of your company (and career) is friendly.

Chapter Summary

- The fundamentals of data will get you far but if you're ready, data science can help you do even more.
- Data science is about predicting the future while data analysis is about understanding the past and present.
- There are four major practical use cases of data science: fraud detection, recommendations, cost reduction, and innovation.
- You need three things before you embark on a data science project: right data, right people, and right projects.
- Remember: the future of your company and career is friendly.

About the Author

Ruben Ugarte is a Data Strategist at Practico Analytics where he has worked with over 75+ companies from 5 continents and all company stages to use data to make higher quality decisions. This includes clients such as Cornell University, Jive, Uberconference, and Circle.

These decisions helped companies lower acquisition costs, save hundreds of thousands of dollars, and reclaim wasted time. In this time, he has seen a wide range of problems that plague companies in their quest to get more value out of their data. From internal conflicts about resources to a general lack of trust in the data, there are pitfalls everywhere that companies struggle to avoid.

Ruben's ideas and work have been featured in industry-leading blogs such as ConversionXL and Openview Labs. He also maintains a popular blog that has been read by over 100,000 readers. He resides in Vancouver, BC, and spends his free time dancing and learning.

Index

OTHER TITLES IN THE BIG DATA, BUSINESS ANALYTICS, AND SMART TECHNOLOGY COLLECTION

Mark Ferguson, University of South Carolina, Editor

- *Emerging Technologies: Blockchain of Intelligent Things to Boost Revenues* by Errol S. van Engelen
- *Data-Driven Business Models for the Digital Economy* by Rado Kotorov
- *Highly Effective Marketing Analytics: A Practical Guide to Improving Marketing ROI with Analytics* by Mu Hu
- *Business Analytics: A Data Driven Decision Making Approach for Business, Volume II* by Amar Sahay
- *Analytics Boot Camp: Basic Analytics for Business Students and Professionals* by Linda Herkenhoff
- *World Wide Data: The Future of Digital Marketing, E-Commerce, and Big Data* by Alfonso Asensio
- *Introduction to Business Analytics* by Majid Nabavi and David L. Olson
- *New World Technologies: 2020 and Beyond* by Errol S. van Engelen
- *Data Mining Models, Second Edition* by David L. Olson
- *Big Data War: How to Survive Global Big Data Competition* by Patrick H. Park
- *Data Mining Models* by David Olson
- *Business Analytics: A Data-Driven Decision Making Approach for Business, Volume I* by Amar Sahay
- *Location Analytics for Business: The Research and Marketing Strategic Advantage* by David Z. Beitz
- *Business Intelligence and Data Mining* by Anil Maheshwari

Concise and Applied Business Books

The Collection listed above is one of 30 business subject collections that Business Expert Press has grown to make BEP a premiere publisher of print and digital books. Our concise and applied books are for...

- Professionals and Practitioners
- Faculty who adopt our books for courses
- Librarians who know that BEP's Digital Libraries are a unique way to offer students ebooks to download, not restricted with any digital rights management
- Executive Training Course Leaders
- Business Seminar Organizers

Business Expert Press books are for anyone who needs to dig deeper on business ideas, goals, and solutions to everyday problems. Whether one print book, one ebook, or buying a digital library of 110 ebooks, we remain the affordable and smart way to be business smart. For more information, please visit www.businessexpertpress.com, or contact sales@businessexpertpress.com.